A Prop...

Clifford Hill is widely regar............ ....
He is an ordained minister, ...t St Mark's,
Kennington (Church of Engl....... ... London, having pre-
viously spent most of his ministry in Inner City areas of
London, including a number of years in the East End.

Dr Hill is known internationally as a preacher, lecturer,
writer and broadcaster. Academically he is both a
sociologist and a theologian.

The Police and Prison services use him as a consultant
on Inner City affairs, specializing in cultural issues, race
relations and violence in society. He directed the
Parliamentary Group Video Enquiry that resulted in the
tightening of the law relating to violent video films.

Today he exercises an international ministry and is
being used by God to announce to the world the
seriousness of the times in which we live and the urgency
with which we have to consider the hope contained in the
Gospel message.

*Books by the same author
available as Fount Paperbacks*

**The Day Comes
Tell My People I Love Them
Towards the Dawn**

Clifford Hill

A Prophetic People

Collins
FOUNT PAPERBACKS

First published by Fount Paperbacks, London in 1986

Made and printed in Great Britain by
William Collins Sons & Co. Ltd, Glasgow

The quotations from the Bible are generally taken from
The Holy Bible: New International Version, Copyright ©
1978 by New York International Bible Society,
published in Great Britain by Hodder and Stoughton,
and used by kind permission.

Contents

PART 1

The Signs of the Times

1.

Widening the Vision

These are exciting days to be a Christian! But they are also dangerous and demanding days.

There can be few people in the Western world today, whether Christian or non-Christian, who are unaware that we live in critical days of world history. The daily news carries ample evidence of worldwide turmoil, violence and disruption. The massive upheavals in the world economy, social structures and political systems underline the transient nature of the age in which we live. The radical changes – economical, social and political – already experienced during the lifetime of comparatively young people in this present generation underline the complexity of the great issues facing us today. The uncertainties of economists, social commentators and politicians in a world of change add to the great sense of insecurity in the present and apprehension for the future.

Christians who are in touch with the wider world scene can hardly fail to note that there is a fresh move of God in our times. The growth of the world Church at this present time is a phenomenon of the greatest significance. Statistics do not usually make exciting reading to anyone except mathematicians, but the statistics for the vast number of new believers becoming part of the Church of the Lord Jesus Christ in our generation reveal a picture that can hardly fail to excite even those Christians who are the dullest and slowest to understand the great purposes of God.

It was while I was working in the East End of London that I

first became aware of the significance of the days in which we live. All the early years of my ministry were spent in the inner-city, poverty-stricken areas of London. I lived and worked and fully identified with the people of the area, who were experiencing deprivation in its many forms through unemployment, social disadvantage, low standards of education, housing and other amenities. The area also suffered all the complexities of an immigrant settlement, with vast numbers of incomers from many different parts of the old British Commonwealth-West Indians from every island of the Caribbean, Indians and Pakistanis, Kenyans, Ugandans and Nigerians, Chinese from Hong Kong and Singapore, Cypriots both Turks and Greeks, and hosts of others.

Besides differences of nationality we had to cope with all the different cultures, languages, traditions and expectations of the mixed multitude who settled among a people already struggling with many forms of disadvantage. We saw church after church close its doors as congregations dwindled when committed Christians moved out of the area and those who remained were unable to cope with the changing demands of mission in the radically changing social milieu. The whole Christian community seemed to be under the influence of a spirit of depression as the "failure syndrome" gripped tightly, and one church building after another became a warehouse, a supermarket, a Sikh temple, or was demolished and the site used for commercial purposes.

Then, in the early 1970s, we began to witness the turning of the tide. Many Christians were starting to experience a new sense of the presence of God through the work of the Holy Spirit in their lives. This gave fresh vision for a renewed Church and a new sense of mission and purpose. We began planting new churches and reopening redundant church buildings as centres of Christian mission, and using new methods of evangelistic outreach and witness that were suited

10

to the needs of the area and its people. Fresh hope, joy and enthusiasm began to replace the spirit of despair as we saw God at work among us, within us, and around us. For my wife and me these were exciting and demanding days. We were totally absorbed in our mission work, despite our family commitments and leadership responsibilities for a large mission staff. Our three children spent their childhood years during this period.

It was for our children that we feared most. We often asked ourselves what we were doing to their lives by our commitment to the work to which we believed God had called us. We had to learn that when God calls you he takes care of every detail, and we had to learn to trust him for those things that were most precious to us, even our own beloved children. Learning to trust for those we loved most meant the realization that God loves our children even more than we love them. It was not simply the problems that arose through the low standards of education in our area that troubled us for our children, or even the constant physical dangers that were all around, but the inevitable conflict they had to cope with through the differences between the values in our home and family life and those they encountered in school and neighbourhood. Peer group pressures to conform from the other children in their lives were enormous and were a constant cause of suffering, both for our children and for my wife and me.

It was during these days that we learned the lessons that God was wanting to teach us in preparation for the coming task. There was the lesson of absolute obedience and the lesson that God is a God who not only takes care of every detail but also ensures that nothing is wasted. This was probably one of the most significant things I had to learn. In the economy of the Lord all our experiences are valuable, even the negative ones, and most of all our failures.

In our mission work with a staff of twenty-two highly

committed, mainly young, Christians we never used the word "failure". We struck it from our vocabulary. We were determined to break away from the failure syndrome that was the malaise of the area. We worked in teams, which specialized in children's work, youth work, work among the elderly, work with Asians and with West Indians. Our teams naturally included members of these ethnic minorities. We were working with churches of all denominations across a wide area of London's East End and Dockland. We saw our task as developing what we called "community based evangelism", strengthening the mission of the local church with our specialist resources and helping to indigenize the Gospel in the area.

There were, of course, many things we tried that were not very fruitful, although we refused to call them "experiments". They were "mission projects". If a project was not particularly fruitful, it was a "learning experience", not a "failure". We learned as much from the things that did not work as from the things that did!

The East End of London is one of the most complex areas for evangelism in Britain. It was this positive attitude towards mission developed there that helped to prepare me for the ministry I am at present exercising. It taught me to be sensitive to people, to be alert to signs of strain among my colleagues and those with whom they were working in the community. It taught me to identify the areas of stress in each neighbourhood and in the different ethnic communities. It taught me the vast potential in the lives of people trapped in the ghettos of deprivation and depressed by the social forces that label individuals and whole communities as being "good-for-nothing". It taught me the liberating power of the Gospel and the incredible things the Holy Spirit can do in the lives of believers through the transforming, renewing, redeeming presence of Christ in their lives. Above all it taught me the limits of my own human wisdom, both in identifying the complex social forces at work and in finding solutions. The incredible complexities of life in the East End defy the most powerful intellect to analyse and resolve. It was in the East End, with my great love for the people and my deep desire to see changes in their lives and the liberating power of Christ setting them free, that I learned not only the limits of my own frail humanity and intellectual ability but also my utter dependence upon God.

Throughout our ministry in the East End I was also involved in the academic world. For seven years I held a post as Senior Lecturer in Sociology, teaching the Sociology of Religion to undergraduates reading for the London University BSc(Sociology) and tutoring postgraduates for MPhils and PhDs in sociology. There were many times when I found the demands of a full-time academic post plus my mission work almost intolerable. Yet I knew God had put me there for a purpose and that he would give me the strength to cope with the pressures so long as it was within his will.

Originally I had taken the academic post out of sheer economic necessity when we had left pastoring a large North London church to go to a tiny East End congregation. We used my salary not only to support the family but also to initiate the work. As others joined us and committed their lives to serving Christ with us we lived by faith, sharing whatever income there was – of which my salary was an important part. The strain of carrying a full-time academic post plus leading our expanding mission team and pastoring a church eventually took its toll on my health, and I succumbed to a serious bout of glandular fever which confined me to bed for two months; it was a year before I was restored to full health.

My doctor, who was a committed Christian and took a great interest in our work, warned me in no uncertain terms that the day had come for me to choose between the academic world and our East End ministry. I accepted my illness as a

13

sign from the Lord that the time for change had come. There was no question of which to choose. Dearly as I loved the academic world and the stimulus of staff room debates with my Marxist colleagues in the Sociology Faculty, and much as I enjoyed tearing asunder the cherished concepts of the young Marxists and budding revolutionaries who faced me each day in the lecture room, I belonged to the Lord! I had been given to him while I was still in the womb and I had been conscious of my calling since the age of twelve.

I left university life with more than a twinge of sadness, but God was good and immediately opened up the way for me to do a little part-time lecturing in sociology and the sociology of religion to Baptist theological students at Spurgeon's College. On one day a week I used to drive over to South London "to bring them a breath of reality from the East End", as I used to tell them. This was a great help to me in keeping my mind stimulated, and it helped a lot of young ministers to understand an area of life of which few of them had any experience.

Losing my academic salary was a blow, both to the ministry and for us personally. We knew that if God removed that source of income he would provide for us in another way. We knew this *in theory*, but it had never been tested! Now our faith was put to the test. I had written out my resignation in great confidence that the Lord would supply. But nothing came. We began to draw upon our slender savings, and as the weeks became months and with every penny of our reserves gone we began to cry out to God more urgently. With three children dependent upon us, my own health still subject to bouts of fever, and my wife fully involved, but unpaid, in our mission work there seemed to be no alternative but to go on trusting that the Lord who had called us would take care of our lives. We told ourselves time and again that he had called, he knew our need, and he was faithful.

My wife and I have never been good at sharing our personal problems with others, and even those closest to us were not aware how near we often were to having insufficient for the basic necessities and food we required. But God always did supply. A gift would come from some unknown donor, or from one of our beloved local people who perhaps sensed our needs or was prompted by the Spirit within to show us a tangible token of their love.

It was a whole year before we were back on a regular salary. With everything gone, and when we had learned to live in daily trust upon the Lord, the telephone rang and a woman whom I had met only once previously some time back said, "I hear that you don't have a salary. Is that correct?" I said I didn't know how she had heard, but that it was true. She said the organization she represented was interested in our work and would like to support me with a salary for the next three years. We rejoiced greatly and thanked God for his goodness and his wonderful faithfulness. Like Paul, we had learned how to live in poverty and in plenty, how "to abound and to be abased".

All this was an essential preparation for the path we were to tread and the ministry I was to exercise. In God's economy nothing is wasted. We had to learn the lessons of absolute trust and obedience. For anyone called to the ministry of a prophet there is no more essential lesson to be learned. The prophetic task is to listen to God, to watch for every sign of his activity, to interpret rightly what he is saying and doing, and then to proclaim with boldness the word of the Lord. It is only God who can give that boldness, for the world despises, scorns and rejects the word of God. Moreover, we live in a day of secularism and unbelief within the Church, and therefore anyone who dares to proclaim the word of the Lord with authority is subject to the fiercest criticism from other Christians; their motives may range from jealousy to sheer unbelief in the present reality of the Living God. Those who think that the ministry of the prophet is something desirable or has an enviable status could not be more mistaken. It is surely the least desirable and most onerous of all the ministry gifts. I have tried many times and in many ways to run away from it, refusing to acknowledge the ministry even when others were affirming the work I was doing and the words I was saying.

It is only God who can give a ministry gift, and he alone affirms that gift and establishes it so that it is recognizable by others. In looking back over my own life I can see how every part of it has been a preparation for the ministry I am presently exercising, even those times when I have not been attentive to God or have been disobedient to him. He uses all our experiences when we are surrendered to him. He takes each part of us, refines it and brings it gloriously into his service. I believe my time in the academic world has been as important a part of preparation as my time in pastoral service or mission work.

One of the great dangers facing Christian leaders today is the limitation of their vision through their commitment to the task of their present ministry. So often we allow the merely urgent to determine our priorities. Ministers in pastoral charge, as well as those with administrative responsibilities, are equally driven by the pressures of the institutional structures around them, the pastoral needs and the local situations for which we carry responsibility. One of the greatest needs in the Church today is for vision; for wider and clearer understanding of the world situation to which we are called to minister and to proclaim the word of God. Christians need to break out of the cocoons and strictures that bind their lives in order to understand the significance of the times to which we live and what God is doing in his world.

I suppose it is an inevitable consequence of our human limitations that it is only the things that are near at hand and absorb our attention for the moment that represent the world of reality for us. The great danger of this is that it can severely limit our spiritual vision and our insight into the significance of contemporary world events within the context of the overall purposes of God. We can fail to understand and appreciate what God is doing in the world, and therefore fail to grasp the significance of what he is saying to us, for God speaks through his deeds as well as through direct revelation.

It is, of course, right and proper that we should be fully committed to our present task, and right that our energies should be totally absorbed in the work to which we have set our hands as the calling of God for our lives. But unless we are able to see that work as part of the overall work of the kingdom, and to see our own task within the context of this wider work, we shall fail to grasp the purposes of God for his people in this generation. It is all too easy to allow our commitment to the immediate task to blind us to the wider world around us. The old saying, "You can't see the forest for the trees" is very true for millions of Christians today, despite the fact that we live in a generation when the worldwide communications network is more efficient and reaches more nations than at any time in past world history. The greatest danger in our inability to see the overall pattern of the forest when we are surrounded by trees is not simply that the density of the trees tends to shut out the light, but that the path we are on may be a circular one, which never in the end leads us out of the forest! We may thus spend our entire lives totally immersed in the humdrum realities that surround us and keep our attention fully engrossed as we move from one urgent priority to the next, so that we never do in fact realize that we are getting nowhere – that our actual measure of achievement is nil. Despite our busyness and declared commitment to God, we are not flowing in the centre of his will and purpose. We are not being carried by the river of life, but rather are being driven by the winds of change generated by a secular society.

The most urgent need in our world today is not for political saviours to exercise charismatic leadership, or scientific geniuses to invent new technology, or economic wizards to devise schemes to solve the world's monetary problems, or social reformers to fight for human rights. That is not to say that these things are not in themselves good, nor that we do not need people with dedication, commitment and a variety of skills, natural talents and spiritual gifts, willing to use their lives for improving relationships between communities, to work to improve the lot of mankind and to establish justice upon the earth. These are worthy causes but there is an even greater and more pressing need in the world today, and that is to hear the word of God for our times. Only God can give us clear directions. We see in part, he sees the whole. We see only the present, but he sees the end from the beginning.

Mankind certainly has great physical needs, for this is a day of massive injustice. It is a day of violence and aggression. It is a day of famine, when millions die for want of food through drought, crop failure, disease and malnutrition. The physical needs of man are multiple and multifarious. But the hunger for bread is not the only pressing need. Man does not live by bread alone but by every word that proceeds from the mouth of God. The spiritual needs of mankind are even more urgent. The spiritual hunger in our generation is the most outstanding need of modern man. Truly there is famine today, but it is famine not for bread but for the word of the living God.

Who can satisfy the deepest longings of man for a right relationship with his Creator, that alone can bring him into right relationships with other created beings and into harmony with the whole natural order of creation? Who can bring the word that will still the warring factions of mankind? Who can bring vision that can lift the eyes of man above the merely material and above the urgent priorities of the demands of daily life? Who can bring release to the captives of the materialistic order of this present generation? Who can set free those enslaved by the secularism of modern society? Who has the power to break the chains and set the captives free?

God alone has the answer to all our needs! He only has the

key to life that can unlock the prison cell of our present predicament and open us up to the wonder of his eternal reality. He alone can penetrate the gloom, smash the darkness and surround us with the eternal light that brings love and joy and peace, that sets the captives free, that places our feet upon a new path where we know ourselves to be in the centre of his will and fulfilling the great purposes of our God, the Almighty, the unchanging eternal Creator whose glory fills the universe and will one day be revealed to the whole created order.

2.

The Threat to the World

There came a point in the ministry of Jesus when opposition to him had grown to such a point that it became dangerous to be with him. A number of those who had followed him during the days of his popularity now began to fall away. Noting this, Jesus one day turned to the twelve and said, "Now what about you, will you also go away?" They replied, "Lord, to whom shall we go? You have the words of life."

The disciples' dilemma was neatly summed up in these words. They, more than anyone, were aware of the danger to Jesus. They pleaded with him not to go up to Jerusalem when the call came from Mary and Martha that Lazarus was dying in Bethany. When Jesus was determined to go despite the threat to his life, Thomas summed up the attitude of them all, "Let us also go, that we may die with him" (John 11:16).

For the disciples there was no one else worth following and there was nowhere else they would rather be than at Jesus' side. They had seen in him the power of God, and they had recognized within him the Spirit of the Living God. They had heard from his lips the words of life – the authentic word of God. Once they had recognized and accepted the real thing everything else would either be second-best or counterfeit.

I remember once travelling many miles across a long, hot, dusty desert in California. Our bodies were rapidly becoming dehydrated in the heat. We stopped numerous times to drink from the bottled water we were carrying, but each time was less satisfying as the heat penetrated the bottles and the water became tepid and stale.

Eventually we reached the foot of a mountain range and climbed some distance until we reached a fast-running mountain stream of pure, clear, cool water. We continued climbing until at last we came to the spring that was the source of the mountain stream, and there we knelt to drink deeply of the pure, clear water that bubbled up through the rock into a gentle pool before beginning its long descent to the plain below. I had never before experienced such an indescribably pure and wonderful taste. For me it was the physical expression of "living water". Having once tasted the real thing I felt as though I never again wanted to drink the constantly recycled city water that is my normal daily diet. It contrasted vividly with the lukewarm liquid we had been drinking from our bottles. When you have once tasted the real thing everything else becomes counterfeit. This was why the disciples could never leave Jesus, even though it meant dying with him. Life without him was nothing.

It is part of the fundamental nature of mankind, according to the purpose of God in creation, to have the capacity to recognize spiritual truth. This does not mean that man is incapable of being deceived – quite the reverse! It is part of man's nature to hunger and thirst after truth, and there is plenty of counterfeit to confuse and delude the most ardent searchers. We live in a day when counterfeit truth is particularly active. Occultism and spiritism in many forms are misleading the multitudes. But the very fact that this is happening is one of the signs of the times in which we live. Jesus warned us that there would be false Christs and false prophets who would appear and deceive many, and that this would be one of the signs of the approaching climax of the age (Matthew 24:4 and 11).

Man's capacity to recognize and respond to fundamental spiritual truth is limited by the extent to which he is enslaved by his sinful nature and the powers of evil that drive him. Paul recognized this problem at the heart of spiritual warfare in

Romans 7, which he summed up in the last verse, "So then, I myself in my mind am a slave to God's law, but in the sinful nature a slave to the law of sin." The spiritual battle between truth and falsity must inevitably reach a peak as we draw towards the climax of the age, because it is the truth that sets men free from the grip of the powers of evil that are driving mankind towards destruction. There is abundant evidence today of the fierce nature of that conflict. It is a conflict that is being waged for the control of the mind and spirit of man. Thus man's hunger and thirst after truth, and his capacity to recognize the truth of the Gospel when there is a clear presentation of the word of God, is limited by the confusion created by the activity of the forces of evil at work in the world. It is rather like a country that is protected by a defensive radar screen designed to give warning of the approach of enemy missiles. The enemy then puts up a multitude of decoys that give false signals on the radar. This creates such confusion that at least a percentage of the hostile missiles do get through the defensive screen.

This is a day when great numbers of mankind are being deceived, when whole nations are being driven by gross distortions of the truth. Never since the beginning of recorded history has the threat to the very survival of mankind been so great as it is today. The threat comes from the twin forces of false religious systems and false political systems. At the milder end of the spectrum of false religions we have various forms of occultism, astrology and witchcraft, while at the more aggressive and militant end we have the spectre of fundamentalist Islam with its Jihad plans to carry out a full-scale "Holy War" against those who are declared to be the "enemies of Allah". The real deception lies in the concept of the nature of Allah, which is fundamental to the false teaching of the Koran. Whole nations are now being gripped and deceived by the spirit of madness that leads to violence, acts of terrorism and mass murder, including the suicide of the aggressors.

In the political arena the mildest forms of Marxism are seen in such countries as Ethiopia, where the misguided leadership actually twist Marxist doctrine to such an extent that their adherents are able to use the resultant power to their own advantage, increasing the poverty as well as the powerlessness of the poor. At the other end of the spectrum is the much more dangerous and aggressive form of Marxism that seeks world domination, and which is epitomized in Bolshevik communism.

The prophecy in Ezekiel 38 refers to the coming together, in some kind of co-operative union, of two great forces of evil and deception. The detail of the prophecy is by no means clear, but it seems to be a fully justified interpretation to link Gog and Magog with two great international forces of spiritual deception – those of false religion and false political systems. The prophecy of Ezekiel 38 is one of the great unfulfilled prophecies of the Bible that deserves close attention today. Most biblical scholars agree with the identification of Russia with Gog, or the Prince of Rosh, the land of the Far North. The "land of the North" in Jeremiah's terminology usually refers to Babylon, but the "land of the Far North" in Ezekiel's usage can have no other interpretation than Russia. Some of the other nations mentioned by Ezekiel in the same chapter are clearly identifiable. Persia is of course Iran and Cush is Ethiopia (verse 5).

The prophecy in Ezekiel 38 refers to a time of international conflict in the Middle East, when several nations will join forces to invade the land of Israel in a period following the restoration of the people to the land after a long dispersion and separation:

In future years you will invade a land that has recovered from war, whose people were gathered from many nations to the mountains of Israel, which had long been desolate. They had been brought out from the nations, and now all of them live in safety. You and all your troops and the many

23

nations with you will go up, advancing like a storm: you will be like a cloud covering the land (Ezekiel 38:8–9).

Verses 10–12 speak of a conspiracy between the attacking nations to "invade a land of unwalled villages . . . a peaceful and unsuspecting people – all of them living without walls and without bars". Modern Israel can certainly not be said to be "a peaceful and unsuspecting people", but it is literally true that for the first time in the history of that land towns and cities have been built without walls and gates. Even Jerusalem today is a city without walls; it has spilled out far beyond the walls of the Old City. If we take the spirit rather than the literal detail of the prophecy it undoubtedly refers to a conspiracy to plan and execute a surprise attack. As such it may well refer to a coming together of the forces of false religion and false politics, with the intention of destroying Israel and utterly annihilating her people.

It is quite possible that such a scheme could be devised in the not too distant future. Once the conflict between Iran and Iraq is finally settled, the Iranian Ayatollahs will be able to turn their attention to their ultimate goal – that of the annihilation of Israel through a Holy War against what is seen as the chief enemy of Allah.

The objective of the Russian leadership is very clearly that of controlling the rich oilfields of the Middle East. It is for this reason that Russia invaded and has doggedly held on to Afghanistan despite almost universal international pressures, including those from the Muslim nations. Afghanistan provides a very convenient springboard for an invasion of the Middle East when the time is right. That time could well depend upon the development of the new militant form of Shi-ite Muslim aggression.

In the generally unsettled condition of volatile Middle Eastern politics that has torn Lebanon asunder in recent years and given rise to dissension between most of the Islamic Middle Eastern states surrounding Israel, if the so-called "Islamic Revival" were to spread right through these states it could provide just the unifying power needed to bring united action and a common policy. This would indeed spell danger of the utmost threat to Israel. If the new Islamic fundamentalists do become the dominant force in the Middle East Arab states, it could well be that a link between Iranian-style Islamic aggression and the Russian ambitions for Middle Eastern political dominance could coalesce.

It seems unthinkable that there could be an alliance between a monotheistic religious system of fanatical believers in a God who controls the destiny of mankind, and an atheistic political system that denies the very existence of any kind of God in the universe. Yet a common cause often brings together the strangest of partners. The Islamic states that have already made two major attempts to destroy Israel, both of which have ended in disaster and defeat, may decide that they need the help of Russia to enable them to achieve their objectives. They would thus enter into a partnership with that object in mind, in the belief that once Israel was destroyed they would be able to shake off the political dominance of Russia and proceed with the worldwide spread of Islam, which is their ultimate objective.

Russia, on the other hand, would enter into a partnership with the Islamic states knowing that such an alliance would be popular with the millions of Muslims who now live in the southern Soviets, and who have been a constant source of irritation and political anxiety to the Bolshevik rulers in Moscow. They would believe that such a partnership with the Arab states would enable them to move their armies freely across the Middle East, and that once established there they would be able to shake off the religious influence of Islam, since they believe that all religion is a delusion, and that as mankind becomes politically and socially mature the desire to hold religious beliefs will disappear. This is a basic tenet of Marxist thinking and strategy. Thus the Russian leadership would be willing to participate in a scheme of partnership that would allow them to achieve their objectives and then shake off the undesirable influence of Islam.

It could well be that the scheme of partnership between Islam and Russia is that which Ezekiel sees when he says, "On that day thoughts will come into your mind and you will devise an evil scheme" (Ezekiel 38:10). The partnership between false politics and false religion would present a powerful combination of evil, such as that envisaged in this prophecy. But the prophecy also includes a warning that fire will descend not only upon Magog but also upon "those who live in safety in the coastlands" (Ezekiel 39:6). In the current usage of that term in the period of Ezekiel, the "coastlands and isles" referred to the lands in the far west of Europe, which was the edge of the then known world. These lands would be Italy, Spain, France, Belgium, Netherlands, Denmark and Britain.

The prophecy of fire descending from on high in a period of tremendous destruction at a time of international conflict is foretold many times in the Bible. Among the most vivid descriptions is that of Isaiah 24, which for centuries has been disregarded by biblical scholars because of its supposed Apocalyptic nature. The worldwide destruction of which it speaks, in which all vegetation is dried up, most of the earth's inhabitants are burned to death and the destructive force is so great that it actually disturbs the crust of the earth's surface – all this was felt to be so far-fetched from reality that the prophecy had to have a symbolic interpretation. Previous generations could not imagine a destructive power being loosed upon the earth that had sufficient force to fulfil the horrific picture of destruction foreseen by Isaiah.

Today we know otherwise! The atomic bombs dropped upon Hiroshima and Nagasaki appear to be mere toys, primitive fireworks, in comparison with the multi-megaton, multiple-warhead weapons now in the possession of the super-powers and soon to become the possession of the smaller states, no doubt including the Islamic fundamentalist Middle Eastern states. When that day arrives there will be no peace for the world; the time will have come when the vision of utter destruction seen by the prophet Isaiah will become a reality.

The day of death and destruction which will rain down upon the nations of the northern hemisphere in the form of fireballs sweeping across the cities, will be followed by what has become known as "the nuclear winter" brought about by the great cloud of particle dust being swept up into the higher atmosphere and substratosphere around the earth. This will blot out the light of the sun for many days and cause the temperature to fall rapidly far below zero. These sub-zero temperatures will spread death and destruction to most of the living creatures and vegetation that survive the holocaust; these same sub-zero temperatures are likely to reach right round the earth, even destroying the tropical forests of Africa. Such would be the consequences of an all-out exchange of nuclear weapons.

Jesus spoke of the days when "the sun will be darkened, and the moon will not give its light; the stars will fall from the sky, and the heavenly bodies will be shaken" (Matthew 24:29). Could that day be near? There are many signs that we have been approaching the days of the fulfilment of Jesus' prophecy. Mankind's greatest need today is not simply to be aware of the danger but to hear what God is saying to us – to heed the word of God for our times.

It is not only the scientists and political leaders who are aware of the great threat to the very future existence of mankind today; among the ordinary people in many nations there is a growing awareness of the danger. That danger is increased by the fanaticism of those who hold false religious and political beliefs, and who are in the grip of forces of evil that drive them towards self-destruction. The evidence that such a spirit of violence and aggression has been loosed in the world today is demonstrated time after time in the news of current events. It is thus for good reason that a spirit of fear and foreboding is gripping people of many nations. Such a spirit of fear underlies the various campaigns for nuclear disarmament, and the so-called "peace movements" that are the reaction of many peoples.

These movements, however well motivated, do not provide the answer, they merely underline the problem. The answer to the dilemma facing mankind does not lie in negotiating pacts and treaties between the nations, but in hearing and heeding the word of God for our time. Only God knows and understands the true nature of the problem facing mankind. He alone knows the heart of man, and he alone knows the true nature of the forces that are at work in the spiritual realms affecting the nations today.

Only God understands the problem and only God has the answer. He alone has the word of life that can overcome the forces of death and destruction. The most urgent task for Christians today is to communicate that word of life to men and women throughout the world, and to the leaders of the nations.

3.

The Prophetic Task

The whole of the Bible bears witness to the fact that God communicates with his people. This communication is not through nature or magic but through man. God speaks through men and women whose spiritual lives are open to him. Abraham is called the friend of God. It was a friendship based upon a two way relationship of communication. Moses spoke face to face with God. Joshua was one who received his orders directly from God, and Gideon was a leader whom men followed because they knew he was hearing from God.

The most outstanding men in communication with God were the prophets, who were regarded not merely as holy men but as the very mouthpiece of God. It was the prophets' task to bring vision to the nation, and to communicate the word of the living God to both leaders and people within the context of the contemporary situation. This often meant speaking words of sharp rebuke. They declared, with a boldness that went far beyond that of human arrogance, what God was feeling and saying about the attitudes and actions of those who were supposed to be his people – people in a covenant relationship with himself. They declared that God hated injustice and oppression, that he could not tolerate religious hypocrisy, that he saw what was happening in private – the lusts and immorality of the supposedly respectable and righteous – that he wept over the faithlessness and lack of trust of his people, that he was warning them in the straightest terms of the inevitable consequences of their actions, but that he nevertheless still loved them and longed to forgive them and have compassion upon them, embracing them with his loving arms of protection.

This was typical of the message brought by the prophets and declared to both leaders and people, wherever the prophets could gather an audience in city streets, in villages and towns, and in the Temple courtyards. This was typical of the message delivered by the prophets with an authority that was part of the anointing of the Spirit of God upon them. It was this authority that was recognized by men who, although they hated the words of rebuke, nevertheless held the prophet in awe. Although the prophets were often abused, ill-treated and beaten, men feared actually to murder them and very few were martyred for their ministry.

The giving of vision was as important a part of the ministry of the prophet as was the declaration of the word of God. It was the prophet's responsibility to open the eyes of the people, and to enable them to have spiritual insight that lifted them above the ordinary humdrum events of their daily lives and let them see things from a wider perspective that would lead to an understanding of the great purposes of God. This wider vision was essential in times of national crisis, when the nation was facing internal corruption, disorder and moral, social, political and spiritual decay. It became a matter of the utmost urgency when times of internal disorder in the family and community life of the nation coincided with a period of international threat from powerful enemy armies. Such a time underlined the truth of the proverb "Without vision the people perish" (Proverbs 29:18; AV).

In times of crisis in the history of Israel God has always raised prophets through whom he spoke to the people. In just over two hundred years, from 730 BC, most of the prophetic books in the Bible were written. This was a period of almost continual crisis – of international threat and internal weakness, faithlessness and corruption. The northern kingdom of Israel fell to Assyria in 722 BC, with the destruction of Samaria, the slaughter of her people and the deportation of survivors. The Assyrians then moved south into Judah, destroying most of the towns and fortified cities, and decimating the land. Only Jerusalem held out, encouraged by King Hezekiah's unswerving trust in the Lord, and the prophet Isaiah's powerful witness. The Assyrians withdrew, and before long were themselves defeated by the rising Chaldean empire, whose armies then marched eastward in a determined effort to subdue Judah. Jerusalem fell in 587 BC after a long seige, and the exile in Babylon began. This ended in 538 BC, when Babylon fell to Cyrus the Persian and the Jews were allowed to return home. During this period, from 730 BC to 520 BC, Amos, Micah, Hosea, Isaiah, Jeremiah, Ezekiel and Haggai all prophesied. Their writings represent the greatest proclamation of the word of God ever given to man through men.

Five hundred years later, when the times of crisis were coming to a climax that threatened the annihilation of ancient Israel and the dispersion of the remnant among the nations of the world for many centuries to come, God sent his own beloved Son through whom he would speak clearly with the nation whom he had anointed to be a "light to the Gentiles". Even Jesus was powerless to turn the hearts of a rebellious people back to God, and thereby to change the course of history. The word of life was rejected and the inevitable happened: the forces of death and destruction closed in upon the nation.

It was not God's will that in AD 70 Jerusalem should be destroyed by the Romans and the nation virtually destroyed. It was his desire that the nation should hear and heed the words of Jesus, "Repent and believe the Gospel for the kingdom of God is near." It was his desire that the people should receive Jesus as Messiah, believe his word, and turn in repentance and loving trust to God, so that through them he could carry out his purposes in the world. With the falling

31

away of Israel God raised a people of the New Covenant – a new nation drawn from many nations – a people who were no people became the people of God (2 Timothy 2:10). To them God continued to speak, and through them he continued to carry out his purposes in the world.

The Bible reveals the nature of God as being eternal and unchanging. He is a God of mercy and compassion who delights to forgive his children and to guide them, to lead them to all good things and to bless them abundantly. In order to accomplish his will and purpose for his people God continually communicates with them; he never leaves himself without a witness in any generation. He speaks to his children.

In the New Testament, after the death and resurrection of Jesus, it was by the outpouring of the Holy Spirit through the believers that God communicated with his people. This had long since been prophesied through many of the prophets, but first through Isaiah. God promised to do a new thing (Isaiah 43:19). He said, "For I will pour water on the thirsty land, and streams on the dry ground; I will pour out my Spirit on your offspring, and my blessing on your descendants" (Isaiah 44:3). This same prophetic promise was made more explicit through Joel:

I will pour out my Spirit on all people. Your sons and daughters will prophesy, your old men will dream dreams, your young men will see visions. Even on my servants both men and women, I will pour out my Spirit in those days (Joel 2:28 and 29).

These words were quoted by Peter on the Day of Pentecost, when he addressed the multi – national crowd in Jerusalem in defence of the disciples. Their strange behaviour following the coming of the Holy Spirit upon them was exciting great curiosity in the streets of the city. But Peter added four words of the greatest significance to the prophecy of Joel. Following the words "I will pour out my Spirit in those days" he added, "and they will prophesy" (Acts 2:19).

Peter remembered Jesus speaking about the coming of the Holy Spirit, whom he called "the Comforter", signifying God's eternal and unchanging presence with his people. In the crowd of people drawn from many lands Peter saw the beginning of the fulfilment of God's promise to pour out his Spirit upon believers from all the nations. Moreover, he saw the real significance of this as part of God's strategy of fulfilling his purpose for the nations. "And they will prophesy", he declared. In other words, they will be a prophetic people!

The coming of the Holy Spirit transformed the company of believers from a crowd of ordinary human beings into the body of Christ – a Spirit-filled body of believers who would continue the work of Christ by bringing the word of God to the world. That is what it means to be a prophetic people. The believers in Jesus would convey the word of the Lord to the people of their times. Just as Jesus was the embodiment of the word of God – the Word made flesh (John 1:14) – so too the believers were to be the embodiment of Christ in order to communicate the word of the Living God to unbelievers.

What we are saying is that it is the intention of God that the Church should be the prophet to the nations. As the prophets of the Old Covenant were the mouthpiece of God to the nation Israel – the people of the Old Covenant – so the believers in Jesus – the people of the New Covenant – are to be the prophetic voice of God, conveying his word to the nations of the world. Under the Old Covenant it was individuals who were anointed with the prophetic word. Under the New Covenant it is the whole covenant people who are anointed with the word of God.

This does not mean that every believer is a prophet. Paul uses the analogy of the human body to represent the Church.

In the human body there are many parts, each having different functions and, as he said, the hand cannot say to the foot "I have no need of you". Each part with its different functions is of vital necessity for the health and wholeness of the body, as well as for the effective carrying out of its tasks. It was for this reason that God gave different ministries and different gifts to individuals within the Church. In addition to the major gifts that Paul lists in Ephesians 4:11 (apostles, prophets, evangelists, pastors and teachers), there are numerous other gifts mentioned in the New Testament. Paul draws a distinction between the ministry gifts and what he calls "spiritual gifts" (1 Corinthians 14:1), which are available to all believers who have received the Spirit of the Lord Jesus.

Throughout the New Testament period all the ministries are seen to function together for the building up of the body of Christ and the maturing of the faith, in unity and love, of the people of God, whose task it is to witness to the world and to convey the word of God to their generation. The prophets functioned as the eyes and ears of the body of Christ. Just as in Old Testament times the prophet stood in the counsel of the Lord to hear from him and to convey his word to the people, so too in New Testament times this was the function of the prophet within the body of believers. Just as God had promised to Moses that he would send prophets to the people, so the fulfilment of that promise was continued for the people of the New Covenant.

I will raise up for them a prophet like you from among their brothers; I will put my words in his mouth, and he will tell them everything I command him. If anyone does not listen to my words that the prophet speaks in my name, I myself will call him to account (Deuteronomy 18:18 and 19).

Long after the writing of the New Testament we find prophets being used by God to speak to the people in the early

Church. In the writings of the Didache and the Patristics there are numerous examples of prophets declaring the word of the Lord, enabling the body of Christ to function as a prophetic people, proclaiming the word of God to the nations.

Today, as the world moves deeper and deeper into times of international crisis, with the most appalling potential for the future of mankind, God is again raising prophets among his people so that the Church may be the prophet to the world, and so that the word of God for our times may be proclaimed from the housetops and published with power and authority to the rulers of the nations in the hearing of all peoples.

God is a God of salvation, not a God of destruction. He so loved the world that he sent his only begotten Son that whosoever believes on him might not perish but have everlasting life. God's intention in sending Jesus was not to condemn the world but to save the world (John 3:16 and 17).

The greatest tragedy today is not that we live in an unbelieving generation. It is not that the world is full of evil men, and that weapons of the most incredible destruction have been placed in the hands of unredeemed and sinful men, unbelievers and God-haters. The greatest tragedy today is that in the times of crisis that have come upon the world, which may well be the prelude to the climax of the age, the Church of the Lord Jesus Christ is an unbelieving and faithless caricature, undeserving even of the name of Christ. Because of the faithlessness and unbelief of the people of God who bear his name, God is unable to use the Church as the prophet to the nations, as is his intention.

The Church should be the watchman to the world. The task of the watchman is to discern the approach of the enemy and to sound the warning to the people so that they may be prepared to resist his onslaught. This is what the Church should be doing today. But how can the nations prepare for battle against the enemy when there is no clear warning sounded by the watchman? How can the nations be saved when those who claim the name of the Saviour do not know his word for these times? How can that word be conveyed with clarity, power and authority through the confusion, disunity and lovelessness in the Church of today? Thus says the Lord to his Church:

> If my people *who are called by my name* will humble themselves and pray and seek my face and turn away from their wicked ways, then I will hear from heaven and forgive their sin and I will heal their land (2 Chronicles 7:14).

*

God is saying to his Church, those who are called by the name of Christ Jesus:

> **You must repent first. If you do not, judgement will begin at the household of God – the household of faith where there is no faith – for I will require this generation at your hands if you do not witness to them through the power of the Holy Spirit that I have made available to you and poured out upon you. I do not expect you to go in your own strength. You must go in my strength, in my Spirit, and proclaim my word, for my word is the word of life that alone can bring salvation to the nations.**
>
> **You are not your own, you have been bought with a price. Now you must carry out my purposes by bringing my word to the nations. You are to be a light unto the nations. Proclaim my word! Proclaim it to the nations! For I am with you, I will never leave you nor forsake you. You are my beloved children, my people whom I have redeemed. Obey my commands and you will live.**

36

4.

Discerning the Word of God

There are many ways of discerning the word of God for our times. The first and most important source of it is, of course, the Bible. Just as Jesus was the perfect revelation of the word of God in human flesh, so the Bible is the perfect written word of God, that can neither be taken away from nor added to. It contains all that is needful for our salvation. In addition to the written word of God we have the spoken word of God through the indwelling power of the Holy Spirit. God still speaks to his servants today, to those who have ears to hear and a mind and spirit open to the Lord. We will say more about this later, but for the moment we want to concentrate upon the way in which the prophets often discerned the word of God through his deeds.

God communicates his word to us through what he does; through his actions. The deeds of the Lord are of great significance in discerning and understanding his word. A major part of the task of the prophets in ancient Israel was to interpret the signs that the Lord sent to them, and which enabled the people to perceive his word.

The prophets were students of the contemporary world. They kept a constant watch upon events within the nation and also among the surrounding nations. They followed with avid interest the news both of the international scene and from all parts of the land. They were interested in what was happening in the family life of the people in villages, towns and cities. They studied the social situation as a barometer of the health of the nation. They talked with the merchants in the market place as well as with those who came to buy, both poor and rich, and studied the economic trends of the day. They kept a close watch upon the latest political intrigues, and maintained contact both with the palace and with the Temple. They also watched carefully for any unusual events in the world of nature, for changes in the weather, for drought, for crop disease, plague or famine.

A good example of the way the prophet used the contemporary events of his day to interpret the word of God to the people, and to force home his message with power, is to be found in Amos 4:6-13. Amos piled up the evidence of what had been happening in Israel through natural disasters and through military defeat, to bring home to the people the message that God was conveying to them. He used events that everyone would have known about, and after each one he added the refrain, "Yet you have not returned to me, declares the Lord":

> "I gave you empty stomachs in every city and lack of bread in every town *yet you have not returned to me*" declares the Lord.

The famine which had struck the land in Amos' day had created shortages of food in every city and town throughout Israel. Even the rich were aware of its effects through the escalating price of food. The poor suffered great hardships, and did not need reminding of the pain caused by empty stomachs. Amos went on to speak about the drought that had reduced the harvest that year, and how some towns had suffered worse than others:

> "I also withheld rain from you when the harvest was still three months away. I sent rain on one town, but withheld it from another. One field had rain, another had none and dried up. People staggered from town to town for water but

did not get enough to drink, *yet you have not returned to me"*, declares the Lord.

The picture of people staggering from town to town in search of water is a vivid one. So too is that of fields drying up for want of rain. The people hardly needed reminding of the consequences of the drought and the scant harvest they had reaped that year, but clearly they had not perceived the spiritual significance of this. Amos relentlessly hammered home the message that God was using the vagaries of nature as warning signs to the people. If they continued to ignore these warnings they would do so at their peril.

It was not only the lack of rain that had reduced the harvest and caused hunger and distress and hardship:

"Many times I struck your gardens and vineyards, I struck them with blight and mildew. Locusts devoured your fig and olive trees, *yet you have not returned to me"*, declares the Lord.

Crop disease and blight had resulted in trees and plants that were reduced in their growth or did not bear fruit that was edible. Anything which survived had been eaten by a plague of locusts that had particularly devastated the fig and olive trees. The locusts had no doubt come from the south, which was the usual desert breeding ground, and had moved into the central plains of Israel, eating every living crop in fields and gardens – the memory of which was all too fresh in the minds of Amos' hearers. But even this was not enough. The prophet drove home his message with relentless persistence:

"I sent plagues among you as I did in Egypt. I killed your young men with the sword, along with your captured horses. I filled your nostrils with the stench of your camps, *yet you have not returned to me"*, declares the Lord.

The plague referred to appears to be associated with a sharp military defeat. This no doubt referred to one of Israel's campaigns against Hazael king of Syria, perhaps in an attempt to retake Ramoth Gilead. In 2 Kings 10:32 and 33 we have a record of some of Hazael's victories against Israel. These had been foreseen with prophetic insight by Elisha, who had wept in the presence of Hazael and gave as the reason for his tears, "Because I know the harm you will do to the Israelites . . . you will set fire to their fortified places, kill their young men with the sword, dash their little children to the ground, and rip open their pregnant women" (2 Kings 8:12).

The military defeats suffered by Israel were evidently so severe that the camps were filled with dead bodies that were the result of both plague and battle wounds. The prophet reminded them of these defeats and ascribed them, not to the enemy, but to God!

Amos rounded off his catalogue of signs by a reference to some catastrophic event that had befallen a town:

"I overthrew some of you as I overthrew Sodom and Gomorrah. You were like a burning stick snatched from the fire, *yet you have not returned to me*", declares the Lord.

Exactly what happened in the devastation that descended upon these people is not known now, but it certainly would have been known to those who were listening to the prophet. He had only to refer to it as an event like Sodom and Gomorrah, and they all knew what he was talking about. He was able to hammer home the message he had been sent to declare, that an even greater catastrophe would befall the whole nation unless they heeded the warning signs God had sent to them. In fact the message was, "Prepare to meet your God O Israel"! God would come among them in judgement; no one would be spared unless they heeded the word of the

Lord and repented. This message was not the opinion of a man. The message the prophet delivered was the word of the Living God: "He who forms the mountains, creates the wind, and reveals his thoughts to man."

Amos had a good sociological understanding of society, and he was well aware of the economic and political forces of his day, but his real strength lay in the anointing of the Spirit of God upon him. It was the power and authority of the word of God dwelling in him richly, that was communicated to the people.

It is a fact of history that the people of Israel did not heed the warnings God sent to them. They disregarded the word of God through Amos, and it was not long before catastrophe struck the nation with the onslaught of the Assyrian armies. This came at a time when one king of Israel after another had been assassinated in political intrigues and coups. The disunity and corruption among the leadership of the nation symbolized the general disorder, the moral and spiritual decay at the heart of the nation.

What happened to Israel was the inevitable consequence of a nation in disarray because of its rebellion against God, a lack of righteousness and trust in him at the very same time as there was a concerted attack from the enemy. To ignore the signs of the times as part of the deeds of the Lord is to commit spiritual suicide; it cuts a nation off from the word of God and exposes it to the onslaught of the enemy, to the forces of death. Just as Amos warned the people of the northern kingdom of Israel, so Isaiah warned the people in the southern kingdom of Judah to take heed of what God was saying to them through the signs of the times. "But they have no regard for the deeds of the Lord, no respect for the work of his hands. Therefore my people will go into exile for lack of understanding" (Isaiah 5:12 and 13).

Isaiah's prophecy of the people going into exile was not, in fact, fulfilled in his own lifetime. It must have been a great joy for the prophet to see his message heeded, and for a spirit of repentance to come upon the people led by King Hezekiah. This was followed by spiritual revival, but Isaiah knew that the effects of this revival would not last long and that his prophecy of exile would one day be fulfilled.

It fell to the lot of Jeremiah to be the prophet in Jerusalem at the time when Judah fell and the city was destroyed. He saw the warning signs clearly and was faithful in proclaiming his message, which grew more and more urgent as the days passed and the day of destruction drew nearer. Jeremiah perceived with penetrating clarity the inevitable end of the path which the nation was treading. The foremost danger came not from the enemy outside the gate but from the enemy within: the moral corruption and spiritual decay at the heart of the nation represented the greatest danger. The signs were clear for those who had eyes to see. Jeremiah highlighted six major faults that spelt death and destruction unless his warnings were heeded and there was real turning and repentance in the nation. They are to be found in chapter seven and they are:

1) False religion
2) Injustice
3) Oppression
4) Violence and murder
5) Idolatry
6) Immorality

There was a widespread belief in Judah that the city of Jerusalem was inviolable because it was the Holy City containing the Temple of the Lord. Jeremiah thundered, "Do not trust in deceptive words and say, 'This is the temple of the Lord, the temple of the Lord, the temple of the Lord!'" This was evidence of the false religion of the day; of those who trusted in the outward trappings of religious institutions rather than in a spiritual relationship with God.

The prophet next hit at the injustice in the nation. He appealed to the people, "Change your ways and your actions and deal with each other justly." This was followed by strictures against oppression: "Do not oppress the alien, the fatherless or the widow." He knew that injustice and oppression were hated by God, who required his people to deal justly with one another. Yet all around him Jeremiah saw lies and deception. God had already bidden him to "go up and down the streets of Jerusalem, look around and consider, search through her squares. If you can find but one person who deals honestly and seeks the truth I will forgive this city" (Jeremiah 5:1). Thus he knew that in a time of growing international danger the religious and economic life of the nation was characterized by chaos and corruption. When lies and deception abound no one can trust the word of another, contracts are broken and the commercial as well as the social life of a nation begins to break down.

Jeremiah next spoke of the shedding of innocent blood, which was a further indication that the social life of the nation was full of violence and murder. When no one trusts his neighbour, and the pursuit of self-interest grips the life of a nation, men will stop at nothing to achieve their own ends. Murder and violence become everyday events. This was what was happening in the life of the nation in Jeremiah's time.

Everywhere the prophet went he saw the signs of idolatry. There were altars to foreign gods on the street corner. The countryside was full of idolatry; the worship of many gods went on in the high places in the country. Even the Temple had many things within it that were the supposedly sacred emblems of other gods, and were signs of the syncretism in the very midst of the elaborate Temple ritual. Jeremiah knew that all the sacrifices of the blood of animals and the vain repetition of prayers were not going to save the nation from the onslaught of the enemy while such spiritual corruption and lack of trust in God lay at the heart of the nation's religious life.

Finally Jeremiah narrowed down his verbal onslaught on the sins of the nation to the home and family. Here he saw adultery, marriage breakdown and disorder within the family, a lack of respect in children for parents, and the signs of general breakdown in family life that he knew indicated something wrong with the very foundations of society. He summed up the word of the Lord:

Will you steal and murder, commit adultery and perjury, burn incense to Baal and follow other gods you have not known, and then come and stand before me in this house, which bears my Name, and say, "We are safe" – safe to do these detestable things? Has this house, which bears my Name, become a den of robbers to you? But I have been watching! declares the Lord (Jeremiah 7:9-11).

Then followed the warning to go and see what had already happened to the northern kingdom of Israel, which God had allowed to be overrun by the Assyrians, to find out what had happened to them because of the wickedness of the people and their lack of repentance, despite the clear warnings of God.

Through Jeremiah God communicated with the people of Jerusalem, warning them that he had already spoken to them time and again but that they had so far refused to turn away from their wicked ways.

I spoke to you again and again, but you did not listen; I called you, but you did not answer. Therefore, what I did to Shiloh I will do to the house that bears my Name, the Temple you trust in, the place I gave to you and your fathers. I will thrust you from my presence, just as I did all your brothers, the people of Ephraim (Jeremiah 7:13-15).

Time and again the prophets of Israel and Judah used contemporary events in their day as a means of interpreting to the people what God was saying to them. They deeds of the Lord were a powerful expression of his word.

In our day there is an urgent need for a clear discernment of contemporary world events so that we may understand the signs of the times and therefore interpret the word of God to the nations. For those who have eyes to see there are two major forces in the world today. They are the forces of evil and destruction that lead to death, and the forces of good and creativity that lead to life. The evidence of their activity in the world may be seen in what we may term "the works of man" and in "the deeds of the Lord". It will be our task in the following pages to examine this evidence.

PART 2

The Works of Man

Introduction

In Part Two of this book, where we are examining "the works of man", we shall draw heavily upon sociological insights. Some readers may find this a bit heavy going but I promise you I have cut out all the jargon of my discipline and have written in plain, simple language, explaining the use of any specialized terms. I do hope you will stay with me through this section and not be in too much of a hurry to get into the good news section which is in Part Three.

I really do believe that it is necessary for Christians to understand what is happening in our world today, so that we are not driven helplessly like a ship without a rudder, out of control in a mighty storm. We are only driven by those forces that we are afraid to tackle; we are most fearful of those things we do not understand. Where there is understanding we are able to bring them before the Lord our God, with calm confidence in his ability to direct us and to overcome those things that seek to harm us.

These three chapters should be read in the confidence of Paul's great declaration of faith:

Who shall separate us from the love of Christ? Shall trouble or hardship or persecution or famine or nakedness or danger or sword? . . . No, in all these things we are more than conquerors through him who loved us. For I am convinced that neither death nor life, neither angels nor demons, neither the present nor the future, nor any powers, neither height nor depth, nor anything else in all creation, will be able to separate us from the love of God that is in Christ Jesus our Lord (Romans 35, 8:37–39).

5.

The Forces of Dysfunction

It is clear even to the casual observer that we live in a rapidly changing world. Even comparatively young people have experienced radical and fundamental social changes during their lifetimes, while elderly people born at the beginning of the twentieth century have experienced not one but numerous revolutionary changes. They have experienced a technological revolution of incredible dimensions, that has moved the world from the earliest forms of aviation to space travel, from radio to communications satellites, from slide-rules to computers, from crystal valves to microchips, from sweated labour to automation, from radio to television, from the age of steam to the age of nuclear power, from the rifle to the bazooka, from the hand grenade to the hydrogen bomb, from cavalry charges to chemical warfare, from infantry battles to laser beams, and from tribal warfare to total warfare. Mankind has seen more rapid, radical and revolutionary changes in the lifetime of its present senior citizens than all the changes that have occurred in the previous generations since the beginning of the recorded history of mankind.

The forces of social change briefly outlined in this chapter we are calling "dysfunctional" rather than "destructive", since their effect is to disturb the existing situation in any given area of life rather than to destroy it. Their effect may be to disturb the natural harmony existing in the social, economic, political, or ecological systems.

This may not necessarily be a bad thing – not all change should be regarded as evil. Many of the changes that have

51

occurred during the twentieth century have accorded great benefit to mankind. The processes of change in themselves are neither good nor bad. They have potential for great good and for great harm; they may be either creative or destructive according to the direction they take, and according to the social and spiritual values controlling them. The forces of social change in themselves are not to be feared but are to be reckoned with.

I want to emphasize that what we are doing in this chapter is by no means intended to be a comprehensive sociological analysis. Indeed, social change is a highly complex area of sociology, and one in which there are divergent and fundamentally opposed theoretical principles. Christians do not need to grapple with the complexities of the debate between Marxists and anti-Marxists in the interpretation of social change phenomena, but it is essential that all thinking Christians should have some awareness of the forces that are at work in our world today and some understanding of their significance. We fear that which is unknown but of whose existence we are dimly aware. When we know what is happening in the world, even if the forces appear to be too great for us and too complex for our full comprehension, we are able at least to perceive the broad pattern of events, and we are thereby able to adjust our own lives accordingly, to give sound advice to others and to pray with understanding. It is, perhaps, this latter that is of the greatest significance, because when multitudes of Christians are praying with understanding there is a directional spiritual force released into the world that is capable of countering the forces of darkness – those forces that Paul calls the "principalities and powers".

It is because so many Christians have very little idea of what is going on in the world that the spiritual powers of evil are having such a field-day in this generation! If the children of light would only take a little time and trouble to study the strategy of the principalities and powers, so that they had some understanding of the forces at work in the world today, they would no longer feel helpless before "uncontrollable" powers that are driving the world towards inevitable destruction.

Christians who pray with understanding, and who act with the wisdom and enlightenment that stems from ultimate truth, are able to release into the world creative forces that can remould nations and change the course of history because, as John puts it, "the one who is in you is greater than the one who is in the world" (1 John 4:4). It is as a small contribution towards this greater understanding of what is happening to our world today that we are pausing to outline, in simple language, the main social forces and processes of change that are driving through most areas of the world today. Underlying each of these social forces can be discerned the spiritual forces of lies, greed and fear that are driving mankind.

International Forces

There are four major international social forces that are driving the world today. They are affecting to a greater or lesser extent every nation and every community, however remote, in every region of the world. These international forces are (1) economic, (2) political, (3) ecological, (4) socio-cultural.

1) **The economic forces** encompass the multitudinous advances in technology, the continually changing methods of production and exchange, and the development of multinational monetary systems, multi-national corporations and the opening up of new markets.

2) **The political forces** are dominated by four major thrusts. The first is that of the expansion of Western-type capitalism, with various forms of democracy. The second is

the development of Marxist/Communist systems, with various types of Socialist societies, mostly producing totalitarian or single-party governments. The third political thrust which can be distinguished in most areas of the world is that of "nationalism". This is particularly to be seen in the younger nations of the Third World, where there is a developing sense of nationhood replacing the old tribal form of society. The fourth political thrust is that of "militarism", whereby nations rationalize their need for defensive systems to protect their internal security against subversive forces and to protect their external boundaries against potential aggressors and thereby build up huge military capabilities. This is the political thrust underlying the arms race that is consuming a large portion of the world's wealth, in the belief that each nation must keep up with others in military potential or even achieve a level of superiority.

3) **The ecological forces** are dominated by four major factors. The first is that of the rapidly diminishing natural mineral resources of the world. Of the nineteen non-renewable natural minerals it is estimated that eleven will be exhausted by the middle of the twenty-first century. They are aluminium, copper, gold, lead, mercury, molybdenum, natural gas, petroleum oil, silver, tin and zinc.

In addition mankind is overfishing the seas, destroying animal and plant life and deforesting the land at an alarming rate. The world's forests are being reduced by an area the size of Switzerland every year. This not only affects the balance of nature but also affects the weather pattern and the health of all living creatures, since the forests are a major source of a life-sustaining atmosphere. Secondly, mankind is creating environmental pollution of the air, the land, the waterways and oceans of the world, also at an alarming rate. The rapid growth of cities means the rapid increase in the production of waste. The third ecological element is that of the population explosion in this generation. During the final twenty years of this century the world's population will grow by a figure greater than the total population of the world was at the beginning of the century. In 1900 the world's population was less that 2,000 million. Between 1980 and the year 2000 the world's population will grow by approximately 2,000 million, to a total of 6,000 million. Accompanying the population explosion are the twin scourges of mankind, those of famine and disease. These two are now killing millions every year.

4) **The socio-cultural forces** are the ideas, social values, philosophies and ideologies that motivate mankind. They link in with the other international forces and penetrate every area of life. The major elements that are clearly discernible today are, firstly, the rise of racial awareness whereby each racial group, especially those who have felt despised and rejected, emphasizes its own roots and cultural heritage. Secondly, there is the rise of sectarianism, which also is one of the ideologies of a pariah people, and, together with racial awareness, feeds into the political force of nationalism. Thirdly, there is the philosophy of secularism, which together with the many forms of cultism which abound today moulds the social values that underlie the lifestyle of vast numbers of individuals and whole communities. They stem from man's insatiable desire to be in communication with the trans-cendental spiritual forces outside his own time-space existence.

Finally, overarching all the socio-cultural forces to be seen in our world today, is the ideology of aggression. The spirit of violence that has been released into the world is discernible in almost every nation and community. In its most unsubtle form it appears in the naked aggression of urban guerrilla forces, terrorist organizations, paramilitary groups and criminal gangs. In its subtler forms it appears in the world of sport, where we admire the aggressive tennis player, the aggressive footballer or the aggressive stroke play of the batsman or ball player or golfer. Even in business life aggressive marketing, management or union practices are all held to be ideals. In the world of entertainment violence ranks high among the diversions that titillate the appetites of men and women, both young and old. The forms of violence vary from the watching of boxing and wrestling, bull fighting and blood sports, to scenes of horrific violence on film and video.

Regional Processes

The regional processes of social change are dominated by two major elements that are today affecting most areas of the world. They are the twin processes of **industrialization** and **urbanization**. In the developing countries these are new processes that are changing the social structure of whole nations; in the Western world they have been with us since the time of the Industrial Revolution.

Industrialization in the more industrially advanced parts of the world proceeds through scientific development and through the application of high technology to production, with the continuing movement towards automation and away from the old labour-intensive methods. The motivation underlying much of this industrial development is that of achieving maximum profitability. In Third World countries where industrialization is fairly new and labour is cheap, production methods do not rely so heavily upon advanced technology.

In Third World countries the social effects of industrialization are often very radical, especially where workers are being drawn into the newly formed cities from simple rural tribal communities. There they experience individual wages for the first time. In industrially advanced societies, where individualism is already an established part of the social order, the effects of high technology and computerized automation are a reduction in the significance of the individual and a further twist in the spiral of de-personalization.

Urbanization as a process of social change is closely linked to that of industrialization. It is a new phenomenon in many of the developing countries; whereas in the Western world it has been in progress for a long time. In Third World countries urbanization is the movement of people into the cities; in industrially advanced societies the movement is out from the city. In Third World countries people are being drawn into the cities from rural communities; in Western nations people are attempting to escape from the Inner City areas of social decay in a movement out to the suburbs and to satellite communities on the fringe of industrial areas, thus forming ever expanding conurbations.

The movement from rural community to city produces significant social changes. It is what Max Weber, the German sociologist, described as a movement from *Gesellschaft* to *Gemeinschaft* types of society, that is, from closeknit communities where each individual is known, and has an identity and significance within a mutually supportive community, to the type of society where there is no sense of community or belongingness offering support to the individual. Hence people suffer a loss of identity and personal significance that often leads to a sense of being lost in the crowd, to a feeling of insignificance, or "anomie", that may even lead to hopelessness, despair and suicide.

Alongside the twin major social processes of industrialization and urbanization there run several allied subsidiary processes such as **bureaucratization**,which is the term given to vast administrative systems that control the complex paraphernalia of advanced societies in which multitudes of individuals are reduced to a number in a filing system or an entry in a computer. Then there is the process of **centralization**, through which the autonomy of local communities and the power of local and regional government is gradually removed and concentrated into the hands of centralized authorities, first on a national basis then on a federal or regional basis, as is happening in Europe today with the development of the EEC and the European Parliament, and may one day lead to a "world power". Then there is the process of **standardization**, an outcome of mass production methods in industry and the drive towards maximum profits. The standard product is cheaper to produce, to package and to market. So we live in standard houses, drive standard cars, wear standard clothes, eat standard food, watch standard television programmes, read standard newspapers and advertisements, and eventually become standard men and women. All these processes reduce the significance of the individual to a mere line on a microfilm, a line that will eventually by erased by a computer's instruction on our departure h run alongside industrialization and urbanization but have an independent functioning of their own are "institutionalization" and "secularization".

Institutionalization is the process through which a simple activity becomes a highly complex institution. For example, in Britain hospitals began as hospices – houses where the sick could come and be nursed by dedicated, caring Christians on a voluntary basis. Today they have developed into the vast institution of a State-run health authority. Institutionalization takes place at every level of human activity. In the world of business and commerce a simple one-man business may become a vast multi-national corporation within a single lifetime.

Even Christian organizations are subject to institutionalization. What begins with the anointed evangelistic ministry of a single preacher may become, in thirty years, a giant international organization of the size of the Billy Graham Evangelistic Association. What begins with a group of believers worshipping God in a house, because they long for the freedom to seek and find the Lord without all the complexities of the traditional church around them, may become, in thirty years, a major denomination, with churches and missions in many lands, constitutions, synods, conferences, appeals, publications, missions, committees, theological colleges and even pension schemes for professional ministers, in exactly the same way as the clergy of the churches they once despised and rejected. That is institutionalization! Institutionalization is essentially a process whereby simple activities adopt, and become adapted to, worldly methods and standards that transform them away from simple task performance into complex organizations. All the denominations, including the Pentecostals, have walked that path. Now the House Churches are heading the same way!

National Structures

The processes of change that we have been briefly outlining affect every part of our lives. Sociologists usually distinguish five major areas of life that are applicable to every nation. These are:

1) **The Family**, which includes all those to whom we are related by birth or by marriage. It regulates our familial relationships, our sexual relationships, our inheritance, and gives us our identity and foundational security in society.

2) **Education**, which is the way we acquire knowledge, or the whole "learning process" which begins in the cradle and ends with the grave. It includes both the informal learning process, by which we internalize the values and behavioural norms of society from our family, peer group, neighbourhood and media, as well as the formal learning we receive through schools, colleges and universities.

3) **The Economy** deals basically with work, production and exchange. It includes the way we earn our living and the way we spend our wealth. It includes the whole production process of food, natural resources and manufactured articles,

and the way in which they are distributed, sold, bought or exchanged.

4) **Religion**, which includes the whole of our belief systems, our cultural and moral values. Essentially it is concerned with the transcendental, with man's attempt to reach beyond his physical environment and time-space limitations. It includes the whole of man's search for eternal truth, and thus embraces both the false teachings of cults and occultism as well as the ultimate truth of God-given spiritual revelation.

5) **Politics** includes the twin areas of law and government. It deals with the making of law as well as law enforcement. Thus political systems, the judicial systems, including the law courts, the police and prison services, are all included.

These five areas of life are relevant to every nation, and enable us to look at the way in which the whole social system in the nation functions. The usefulness in looking at national life in this way is that we may examine the effects of the processes of change sweeping through our world today. These processes are bringing about fundamental changes in the life of each nation although, of course, the pattern and effect varies from country to country.

In the highly industrialized and urbanized nations of the Western world, all five of these major areas of life have been changing fundamentally throughout this century, and especially since the 1950s when the rate of change began to accelerate fiercely. There is a basic law in sociology that where one of these major areas of social life, or "social institutions", experiences a basic change, all the others are affected. Hence when the methods of production changed in the economy during the Industrial Revolution, all the other areas of life were affected too. Families were drawn from simple village communities to complex urban life. This changed the method of education and necessitated the introduction of formal education. It brought about the need for changes in law and government to meet the new demands of an urban industrial society, and it brought changes in moral values and beliefs.

In the present period of rapid social change, all our social institutions are generating change from within and are thus affecting each other. The combined effect is rapid, radical and revolutionary change sweeping through society in every nation. Changes in attitudes towards birth control, the rearing of children and discipline have brought about the basic changes in the family, as well as reducing the size of the average family, and throwing an ever-increasing emphasis upon the individual rather than upon the family unit. This has affected all the other areas of life, especially education and the economy. Changes in the law on divorce and abortion have affected the family. Changes in the methods of education and in the exercise of discipline in schools have affected our social values, moral code and beliefs. What is taught in schools influences the openness of children and young people towards religion. The introduction of new methods of production in the economy and advances in technology have not only contributed to greater wealth but also to higher levels of unemployment, which in turn have affected the family and every other area of social life.

All these changes are accelerating, as each change brings about other changes in other areas of life within each nation. Moreover, as communication between the nations grows through the media and increased trade and travel, the changes within each nation affect other nations. There comes a point where the rate of change and the accumulated effects begin to affect the social stability and health of a nation.

Nations have many of the characteristics of the human body, with its different parts each with their own unique functions. After all, nations are made up of people and are in the last resort simply the aggregates of the people who compose them. Just as the human body is affected by changes in the environment, climate or diet, and is also subject to the more subtle psychological pressures of fundamental changes that come about through the death of a near relative or marriage partner, through unemployment or change of job, through moving house, or examination success or failure – in the same way a whole nation is affected by the fundamental changes that occur in its social life.

Each human being has a different capacity for absorbing the impact of changes in his or her life. But there is a point beyond which each one cannot absorb change without impairing his health and stability, and to go beyond that point may well cause a breakdown. If a man loses his job, his wife or children are killed in an accident, and he is forced to give up his home, all within the space of a few months, he is likely to suffer a physical or mental breakdown. His capacity to cope with fundamental changes in his life has been over-reached.

Nations, similarly, have a capacity for absorbing changes in each area of their social life, beyond which they cannot cope without it radically affecting the health and well-being of society. Nations can also suffer breakdowns in their social stability. What we are seeing in many parts of the Western world today is a shaking of the nations which is fundamentally affecting their health and stability. Unless there is a slowdown in the rate of change the number and extent of actual breakdowns will increase. As each one occurs it will affect the life of other nations, and thus the instability of worldwide international relationships will be increased.

God has warned us many times through the prophets concerning the "shaking of the nations" that is occurring in our generation. The rate of change shows no sign of decreasing in the Western world, and there is an accelerating rate of change in the developing nations and among many of the major nations of the East, such as China and Japan. When we consider this, together with the economic and political instability of many nations in the Middle East and Africa, it is not difficult to predict a continuing and prolonged period of world instability. These are the conditions in which re-volutions and counter-revolutions, regional and international wars, all occur.

This is what the Lord Almighty says: "In a little while I will once more shake the heavens and the earth, the sea and the dry land. I will shake all nations" (Haggai 2:6-7).

6.

The Forces of Destruction –
Materialism

The present world situation is compounded by two major destructive *spiritual forces* that are much in evidence today. These are **materialism** and **secularism**. They represent the greatest threat to the stability and even the very future existence of the nations because of the timing of their release into the world. These spiritual forces of evil and destructiveness are undermining every human attempt to stabilize social situations, to slow down the rate of change and to promote harmonious relationships within families, within communities, within nations and on an international level. Their effect can only have the most profound significance and grave consequences for the future of mankind unless their nature is recognized and understood, and effective counter-measures are undertaken as a matter of the utmost urgency.

Perhaps the greatest danger facing mankind is that of delusion. Even Christians have very little understanding of the nature of spiritual warfare. Most teaching on the subject is at a very personal level; it deals with spiritual matters within individual lives and fails to deal with the broader issues. We need to catch a glimpse of what Paul is talking about when he refers to the activity of the "principalities and powers" or the spiritual forces of evil that have been released into the world and are driving the nations. Never was there greater need for a theological understanding of these vast spiritual issues affecting the health of whole nations and threatening to plunge the world into the abyss of self-destruction. Paul's warnings need to be heeded. He declares, "For our struggle is not against flesh and blood, but against the rulers, against the authorities, against the powers of this dark world and against the spiritual forces of evil in the heavenly realms."

Secular man has no understanding of spirituality, and therefore is totally ignorant of what is going on in the spiritual cosmos. So long as Christian teachers and preachers are content to concentrate upon the personal aspects of spiritual warfare they are trivializing the word of God and are in danger of misleading the flock and failing to feed the sheep with the real nourishment of the Gospel. Evangelicals have fallen into this trap for generations.

It is, of course, right to preach the individual basis of salvation. Conversion is not a social process. We must each come by our own decision to receive salvation through trusting Jesus as Lord and Saviour. But conversion is not the end, it is the beginning. God's desire is not for each of us, as individuals, to be alone in the Kingdom, but for the whole family of mankind to embrace the Gospel and enter the Kingdom. Just as he wants us to have a wider vision of the Kingdom and of his great purposes for the salvation of mankind, so God is longing for us to understand the wider significance of the spiritual forces at work in our world today. He has given us in his word all the teaching we need, if we will only allow our minds to be open to his Holy Spirit and if we will open our eyes to perceive what is happening in the world today.

The nations are being driven by destructive forces of evil that emanate from the arch-enemy of mankind. The twin spirits of materialism and secularism combine to blind mankind to the true nature of the danger facing the world. *Materialism keeps us bound to the earth, and secularism blinds us to spiritual reality and tells us that there is no God.*

The Communist Nations

It is plain to see that these are the twin driving forces behind Communism. The Marxist philosophy of dialectic materialism, that sees the key to the interpretation of history as being rooted in the economy and processes of economic change, is essentially materialistic in its basis. It sees economic change as the mainspring of social creativity, and the only way to bring salvation to the people.

Communism is essentially secularist; it has no place for spiritual reality in its system. Marx and Engels took the view that religion is a delusion of the untutored masses, out of which they will grow as they come to social maturity. Marx saw religion as a tool of social control in the hands of the powerful, which enabled them to keep the masses politically and economically enslaved. He taught that religion is the opium of the people, the sigh of the hard-pressed under the yoke of enforced labour.

Thus in Communism the spirit of secularism and the spirit of materialism come together and are fused into a materialistic and secularist philosophy that believes in violent political revolution as a means for achieving its aims and objectives. It holds to the belief that any means are justified by the end. Its objective is to wrest power from the entrepreneurs and place it in the hands of the proletariat, in order that the means of production, and therefore the source of wealth, shall be in the hands of the people.

The great delusion of Communism is that material prosperity and possessions are of ultimate worth and, if more evenly distributed, bring health, wholeness, happiness and well being to mankind.

The failure of Marxism is clearly seen in its practice in Russian Communism. The Russian Revolution did not place power in the hands of the people, neither did it achieve the even distribution of wealth. It simply replaced one group of élites with another; one class of privileged persons with another, for the traditional aristocracy of Tsarist Russia was replaced by the Bolshevik "aristocracy" of Communist Party members who exercise power in such a way as to give themselves maximum privileges in an unequal society.

The secularist philosophy that blinds men to spiritual truth, and sees the physical world as the only reality deludes the rank and file in Communist societies into believing in a form of "social Darwinism", out of which evolutionary process the just society will eventually evolve. It blinds men to the truth that man's nature is essentially selfish, greedy and violent; that the human heart is a great deceiver; and that the just society can only come about when men and women have been justified by the Spirit of the Living God, who alone can change the nature of man.

Communist nations are thus driven by the spiritual forces of evil that are gaining momentum in the modern world, and which are driving the nations towards inevitable destruction.

The Western World

The twin evil spirits of materialism and secularism are also at work in the Western world. Materialism is gaining momentum and deceiving millions. Even Christians are subject to the same spiritual forces of evil, and are liable to be deceived unless they are alert to the true nature of the battle being waged in the heavenlies for control of the world. Many Christians do not recognize the extent to which the forces of evil have already penetrated Western society. They believe, for example, that the Western form of democracy (the dominant political system) and Western capitalism (the dominant economic system) are inseparable and are part of the God-given, divinely blessed order of society. This is a lie, a snare and a delusion. Democracy and capitalism are not inseparable. Capitalism can be practised equally well in a totalitarian, one-party political system, as a number of African states are proving today!

The thing that so many Christians are failing to recognize is the extent to which modern capitalism has changed since its early days at the time of the Reformation, when it was strongly influenced by the preaching of the great Reformers of Europe. It was rooted in a theology of the ultimate worth of each individual before God. But the form of "megacapitalism" that has developed today cares nothing for the individual! Indeed, it will drive him out of business! It has no concern for the little man. Its objective is to build up great multi-national corporations, and to eliminate every competitor in the ruthless and insatiable lust for greater profits.

What we are seeing at work in the Western world are forces that are undermining the worth of the individual, and devaluing him in the eyes of the world and making him feel of no worth. Only the Spirit of God can break the power of the spiritual forces of evil that are driving the nations. We urgently need the Gospel of the Lord Jesus Christ to liberate us from these destructive forces and to set the captives free.

The great forces of the economy that are at work today in both capitalist and totalitarian states care nothing for the poor and powerless. We Christians too are being influenced and driven by the same spirit of evil to a very great extent, so that we are not really caring for the poor or hearing the cries of the oppressed. We are not raising our voices on their behalf or actively standing with them.

God is always on the side of the poor and the oppressed! "When Israel was in slavery I loved him", says the Lord. But when the people of Israel became puffed up and full of greed and oppression God was against them. The prophets speak of the true righteousness of the people of God, and roundly condemn the lack of justice in the nation as being a form of unrighteousness in the eyes of the Lord.

In Isaiah 58 the prophet speaks about the religious life of

the nation, showing that it is a nation full of immorality and unrighteousness, full of lies and deception, full of injustice and oppression. The prophet pours scorn upon the religious righteousness of his day. He asks what is the use of performing religious acts and having fast days when the moral, spiritual and social life of the nation is full of corruption and unrighteousness:

"Is not this the kind of fasting I have chosen," says the Lord, "to loose the chains of injustice and untie the cords of the yoke, to set the oppressed free and break every yoke?
"Is it not to share your food with the hungry and to provide the poor wanderer with shelter – when you see the naked, to clothe him, and not to turn away from your own flesh and blood?"
Then your light will break forth like the dawn, and your healing will quickly appear; then your righteousness will go before you, and the glory of the Lord will be your rearguard.
Then you will call, and the Lord will answer; you will cry for help, and he will say: "Here am I" (Isaiah 58:6-9).

The Western nations today are in danger of coming under the same condemnation as Israel in the time of Isaiah. The forces of materialism are driving so strongly through the Western world that we do not even realize the extent to which our values and our actions have been influenced by them. The greed, selfishness and acquisitiveness that accompany a materialistic obsession blind us to the needs of others, and deafen our ears to the cries of the poor and the hungry. Even when their needs are brought before us by our sophisticated communication systems we turn our heads and pass by on the other side.

The nations of Europe spend hundreds of millions of dollars every year in storing their food surpluses. The grain mountains, butter mountains, meat mountains and wine lakes are a scandal and a scourge, that will one day bring judgement upon the Western world. In 1984 the American grain harvest was reduced by 20 per cent on the order of President Reagan. In the same year six million people died of starvation in Africa, and worldwide ten million children died of hunger and malnutrition. When a nation is more concerned with keeping up the price of grain on the world market than with obeying the Lord's commandment to feed the hungry and to care for the poor and those suffering from the oppression of poverty, that nation is in rebellion against the word of God and will come under judgement. When nations are more concerned with preserving their economies than becoming righteous nations in the sight of the Lord, they have clearly ignored his commandment to "seek first the Kingdom of God and his righteousness", and they have forgotten his promise that "all these things will be added unto you" – all the material blessings will follow if the pursuit of righteousness and the values of the Kingdom of God are placed foremost in the life of the nation.

Hear the word of the Lord, you nations of the West!

Your iniquities have separated you from your God; your sins have hidden his face from you, so that he will not hear.

For your hands are stained with blood, your fingers with guilt. Your lips have spoken lies and your tongue mutters wicked things.

No one calls for justice; no one pleads his case with integrity. They rely on empty arguments and speak lies; they conceive trouble and give birth to evil . . . . Their deeds are evil deeds and acts of violence are in their hands.

Their feet rush into sin; they are swift to shed innocent blood. Their thoughts are evil thoughts; ruin and destruction mark their ways.

The way of peace they do not know; there is no justice in

their paths. They have turned them into crooked roads; no one who walks in them will know peace (Isaiah 59:2-4, 6b-8).

In a recent national survey in America something like 90 per cent of those interviewed said they believed that if they had a 25 per cent increase in their income and level of wealth they would be happier. Thus the great majority of the American people have swallowed the lie that material possessions bring happiness. This is the basic fallacy of a materialist philosophy: it convinces us that material possessions are the most important things in life. The lack of them makes us feel deprived; we behave like spoilt children, saying that life is unfair and demanding more.

The most interesting thing about the American survey is that it was not just the poor who were expressing these views; but those who were comparatively wealthy also believed that to have more would give them greater happiness. The Ethiopian peasant facing a slow death by starvation would settle for a survival diet. The hungry millions in Third World nations would be glad to be able to produce sufficient for subsistence for themselves and their children, but the materialistic philosophy of the rich nations of the Western world demands more and more. It is never satisfied! It has a voracious appetite for the acquisition of material possessions. It continually casts green eyes of envy upon its neighbour and says, "I want! I want! I want more!"

The American dream of owning a fine house with a swimming pool, two or three cars and a log cabin up in the mountains, has been fuelled by vast advertising programmes, all based upon the ethic of acquisitiveness. It has been further fuelled by the vast number and range of television games programmes giving away material prizes in gambling games, guessing games, and as rewards for trivial general knowledge answers. The prizes range from domestic gadgets to cabin cruisers, from holidays in Hawaii to Cadillacs and dream houses; the contestants competing with one another in their displays of exuberant emotion in their joy at winning some new material possession.

Thus the lie is fostered and fed, that more and more means happier and happier. Happy are those who have, for they shall have more. Happy are those who have more than their neighbours, for they shall rejoice greatly. Happy are the rich, for they shall have their heart's desire. Happy are the wealthy, who are able to despise the poor. That is the Western materialist philosphy.

But what did Jesus say? "Blessed are you who are poor, for yours is the Kingdom of God. Blessed are you who hunger now, for you will be satisfied" (Luke 6:20 and 21).

Not all Americans, of course, are wealthy. America is two nations – the "haves" and the "have nots". The tragedy is that all too often the haves are not aware of the plight of the have nots. The materialistic philosophy has so taken hold of the nation that those who have "made it" (materially) from among the poor, despise those who have not. The physical environment has so been manipulated and adjusted that the poor are discreetly tucked away in their own ghettos of poverty so that the rich do not have to observe them or be made to feel guilty whilst enjoying their own lifestyles.

The problems of getting from the outer salubrious suburbs to the business and commercial heart of the city centres without observing the plight of the poor in Inner City slums and undesirable industrial areas has been neatly solved by building elevated motorways over unpalatable areas. Rich Americans can drive from their comfortable homes, in their comfortable air-conditioned cars, to the comfort of their offices, over the roofs of the houses of the poor without even being aware of their existence.

"Lord, when did we see you hungry and thirsty or a stranger or needing clothes or sick or in prison and did not help you?"...

But the Lord replies, "Whatever you did not do for one of the least of these you did not do for me" (Matthew 25:44 and 45).

And the other rich nations of the Western world look with envy upon America, the richest nation of them all, and they say, "If only we were as rich as they are, we would be happy! If only we had a· 25 per cent increase in our gross national product, if only we had a little more, we should be happier", and they too ignore the cries of the world's hungry as they focus their envious attention upon their richer neighbours.

"We want more! We want more!" More possessions mean greater happiness. And the arch-enemy of mankind rubs his hands with glee as the driving force of materialism gains momentum among the nations, for he knows the end result of those who are driven by materialism, whose God is their belly and whose end is destruction (Philippians 3:19).

7.

The Forces of Destruction – Secularism

Accompanying the force of materialism is that of secularism. The two are closely allied; together they form a powerful driving force of evil that is moving throughout the nations of the world today. It is not only in the Communist nations that secularism holds sway. In the Western world, among nations that have had the Gospel for centuries and whose national constitutions have been rooted and grounded in the word of God, there is widespread unbelief, to such an extent that in some there is even a lack of a basic "God-consciousness". Once that point is reached evangelism becomes almost impossible. For the preacher to be able to bring the Gospel with power to unbelievers, a precondition is that there is among the hearers at least a recognition of the existence of a Supreme Being. Without that, however eloquent the presentation of the Gospel may be, it will not result in men trusting the Lord Jesus as their Saviour. Where there is no consciousness of sin men have no use for a Saviour.

In a secular society, where men are blinded even to the existence of God, they must be confronted with the irrefutable evidence of the presence and power of God. This does not come from eloquent preaching. Neither does it come from gentle persuasion or erudite argument. It comes from the prophetic proclamation of the word of God, with power and authority that cuts like a two-edged sword through the clouds of unbelief. It comes from the signs and wonders that inevitably follow such a faithful standing upon the word of God, when the zeal of the Lord is as a consuming fire within the servants of God.

In a secular society the prophetic word of God acts in the same way as a plough that goes ahead of the sower. It breaks up the hard ground and prepares it, so that the ground is receptive when the seed is sown. The prophets of Israel were used by God to break down the hardness of heart among the people when there was widespread turning away from him, and a lack of a right relationship with God and right relationships within the nation. The prophets thundered the word of the Lord with a power and authority that cut through even the scornful unbelief and deliberate rebellion of those who, by their actions, were denying the very existence of God. They proclaimed the word of God with power and authority; they delivered their warnings of impending judgement upon a nation in apostasy before God. As John the Baptist went ahead of Jesus to break up the hard ground and to call men to repentance, so the prophetic word of the Lord needs to be proclaimed among the secular nations today, to turn men away from trusting in man and to prepare the way for trust in God.

We ought at this point to define what we mean by "secularism". Secularism is not a social process, it is an effect. It is what happens to a society subjected to a prolonged period of social change under the impact of secularization. Now secularization is a highly complex social process, and it would be out of place and would break the flow of the Spirit to try to deal with it here. I have written about secularization elsewhere (*The Day Comes*, chapter 12). Our concern here is to understand the force of secularism that has gained a powerful hold upon many nations in the West and is moving strongly throughout the world.

Secularism breaks down the God-consciousness of people and removes the God-context of individual, community and national life. The seriousness and significance of this lies in the effects upon the attitudes and behaviour of people. It removes the divine sanction underlying morality, and thereby removes the basic legitimization of law. Law becomes a mere human legal requirement, rather than the Divine imperative to moral behaviour. Thus the over-arching Divine sanction and authority in the life of a nation is removed by secularism.

This does not mean that men believe nothing. Indeed, the effects of a massive injection of secularism into the life of a once God-fearing nation is not that of a spiritual vacuum. When men cease to believe in God they do not believe nothing – they believe anything! Hence occultism, spiritism and all kinds of superstitions grip the minds and imaginations of men and women, distorting the truth, filling them with fear and fanciful ideas that bind and enslave them, that twist and corrupt their minds and spirits. The evidence of this is everywhere to be seen in the nations of the Western world, where magazines, books and films proliferate on the themes of witchcraft, spiritism and horrific violence. The subject of horror and violence has a preoccupation and fascination for millions in the secular nations of the West. Films depicting scenes of the utmost depravity and explicit sadistic violence have enormous popular appeal. This is an indication of the level to which the minds of men and women have been influenced, and their values twisted, by the spirit of secularism driving through the nations.

Although it is only a minority who practise satanism and actually worship the powers of evil, vast multitudes are, in fact, driven by the same spirit of evil. This is seen, not simply in the superstitions of the masses, the popularity of horoscopes, astrology and the proliferation of all kinds of cults, but it is to be seen in the behaviour of ordinary people. The vast increase of violence in society, in almost every nation throughout the Western world, is one of the indicators of the extent to which the spirit of secularism has been undermining the Divine authority of law in the minds of the ordinary people. "Where there is no revelation, the people cast off restraint" is the NIV's translation of Proverbs 29:18, more popularly known in the AV as "Without vision the people perish". Its meaning undoubtedly is, that where there is no proclamation of the revealed truth of the word of God the people cast off all restraint; they are driven by the basest forces in human nature that eventually lead to self-destruction.

Violence is one of the major characteristics of our age. It is to be seen, not only in the gross international acts of genocide through war between the nations and through the preparations for the nuclear holocaust, such as the stock-piling of 60,000 nuclear weapons, each of which make the bomb that destroyed Hiroshima look like a firework; it is also to be seen in the vast increase in international terrorism. It is to be seen in the urban guerrilla warfare waged by those whose political ambitions are frustrated by democracy, and who believe they can achieve their objectives through terrorizing the innocent and forcing governments into submission. They believe that murder, maiming and mayhem are justified in the pursuit of whatever happens to be their particular cause.

The spirit of violence is also to be seen in communal acts such as street riots, fighting among football fans, vandalism, hooliganism and the general acts of lawlessness that abound in modern Western cities. This spirit of violence is part of the effect of the driving force of secularism that is gaining momentum throughout the world today. It undermines traditional morality, and thereby removes the constraints upon behaviour that hold in check man's baser drives of selfishness, greed and destructiveness. Once the constraints are removed and these forces are released, every area of life – from the family, neighbourhood and local community to the world's international affairs – is affected.

One of the major results of secularism is the redefining of norms and the gradual pushing out of the parameters of

77

decency and moral behaviour. Things that shocked the average Western citizen ten or fifteen years ago are now regarded as normal everyday behaviour. This rapid change in cultural norms is a modern phenomenon. It is a result of the massive changes in technology that have affected communications. Television, advertising, films, video, cable TV, newspapers, magazines and books all contribute to the rapid communication of changing standards of behaviour and moral values among people. Inevitably it is the lowest common denominator that is communicated and which becomes the norm.

When everything is changing there are no fundamental values – no yardstick by which to judge what is good, or what will promote the health and well-being of the community. Thus it is the latest fashion that catches on, the most outrageous form of behaviour that titillates the appetite and becomes the popular fad of the moment. Pop music, hairstyles, clothing and public behaviour are all affected by the media of communication that rapidly transmit right into our homes that which is happening on the other side of the world.

The mass media transmit the opinions and behaviour of the popular heroes of the moment throughout the world, and especially to young people, whose own norms, moral values, beliefs and attitudes are not firmly grounded but are easily influenced and moulded. A process of redefining behavioural norms takes place, that disguises their true nature. Modern man is expert at this, he changes a name and thereby redefines moral values and behaviour. For example, there has been a massive shift of opinion in regard to homosexuality during the past two decades. Homosexual practice used to be illegal in most Western nations, but within a single generation it has been made socially acceptable and its true nature disguised by redefinition. What the Bible calls "sodomy" was changed to "homosexual", and then this in turn was dropped in favour of the term "gay".

We no longer call something by the name which reveals its true nature. We do not speak of men "committing sodomy", or men who are "sodomites", but we refer to them as being "gay", which makes them sound carefree and happy and liberated in their behaviour. In fact this is a complete reversal of the truth! As any pastor or social worker who has worked with homosexuals knows, they are the most miserable, fear-ridden, insecure, inadequate and pathetic members of the community. They were anything but gay even before the onslaught of the AIDS disease. Now that that has hit them, they are of all men the most miserable. You cannot go against the law of God without suffering retribution. The practice of sodomy was responsible for the holocaust of Sodom and Gomorrah. It is an offence against the basic natural law of creation and is abhorrent in the sight of God.

It is not only homosexuality that has been redefined; so too has almost every area of personal moral behaviour. The edge has been taken off fornication and adultery, and now we speak about "sleeping with" and "living together". We never use the term "illegitimacy" or speak about "sexual promiscuity". Instead we speak about "one-parent families" and "libertarian lifestyles" to disguise adultery and marriage breakdown in family life. We speak about "girlie magazines" and "soft porn" which obscures the true identity of obscene publications that exploit girls, degrade women and feed the appetites of lustful, violent men which inevitably explode in wicked behaviour such as rape and violence in the community.

When men redefine moral behaviour in such a way as to obscure its sinful nature, they are in fact breaking the law of God. This is nothing new. It was roundly condemned by the prophet Isaiah back in the days of Hezekiah, when the Assyrian armies were threatening to over-run Judah. Isaiah saw how moral decay and corruption were festering in the nation, undermining the spiritual strength and openness to

79

God that alone could guarantee the nation's defence and security in a time of international threat. He exposed those who were redefining evil as good, with the penetrating prophetic insight that came from the anointing of the Spirit of God upon him.

> Woe to those who call evil good and good evil, who put darkness for light and light for darkness, who put bitter for sweet and sweet for bitter.
> Woe to those who are wise in their own eyes and clever in their own sight.
> Woe to those who are heroes at drinking wine and champions at mixing drinks, who acquit the guilty for a bribe, but deny justice to the innocent.
> Therefore, as tongues of fire lick up straw and as dry grass sinks down in the flames, so their roots will decay and their flowers blow away like dust; for they have rejected the law of the Lord Almighty (Isaiah 5:20-24).

With the same spirit of God upon him as moved Isaiah, Paul saw with prophetic insight the end result of the forces of secularism driving through the nations. He saw what happens to a people who once believed in God and then deliberately rejected his law and rebelled against his word. He wrote:

> Since they did not think it worth while to retain the knowledge of God, he gave them over to a depraved mind, to do what ought not to be done.
> They have become filled with every kind of wickedness, evil, greed and depravity. They are full of envy, murder, strife, deceit and malice. They are gossips, slanderers, God-haters, insolent, arrogant and boastful; they invent ways of doing evil; they disobey their parents; they are senseless, faithless, heartless, ruthless.
> Although they know God's righteous decree that those

who do such things deserve death, they not only continue to do these very things but also approve of those who practise them (Romans 1:28-32).

The secularist/humanist philosophy that seeks to break down traditional morality, and undermines or scorns belief in God, attempts to eliminate sin and thereby to liberate man from what it sees as the binding forces of tradition and religion. However much we attempt to redefine human behaviour and change attitudes towards morality, we cannot change the fundamental laws of the universe that govern human behaviour. They operate in the same way as natural law controls the natural order of creation. Sin defiles man, separates him from God and disturbs his right relationships with others. This inevitably brings hurt and a lack of health and wholeness in the lives of individuals, families and communities.

The secularist/humanist philosophy puts its faith entirely in man and in human ability to solve everything and to create the conditions of happiness, harmony and wholeness in life. In fact, as the abundant evidence of modern secular society demonstrates, the freedom from constraint for which men strive results not in true liberty but in a libertarianism and licence to pursue self-interest, regardless of the cost to others. It thus increases the hurts and suffering among humanity, including the suffering of the innocent; for example, the harm to little children when the sinfulness of their parents results in the breakup of the family, and the disturbance and insecurity of the children. In Britain one thousand children every week suffer the trauma of a broken home through the breakdown of their parents' marriage. In the USA and other Western nations that figure is multiplied many times. It is a tragic commentary upon the deception of secularism that men believe they can have liberty and freedom without any reference to fundamental values and to the standards of righteousness or right relationships established by the Creator of mankind and given to us in the word of our God. When man deliberately rebels against God and rejects his law, he suffers the inevitable consequences; he is driven by the forces of destruction that we see at work in the world today, and which are rapidly gaining momentum as they take an ever firmer grip upon the nations of East and West, North and South. These forces are aided and abetted by the sinful ambitions of men, the selfishness, greed, avariciousness, corruption and violence that are eating like a cancer into the heart of the nations, and are promoted by the ease of communications and international travel.

The writing is upon the wall, not just for the Communist nations who are in the grip of blatant forces of secularism, but also for the nations of the West who have rejected the word of God. They have thereby turned away from his law and are moving out from under his covering protection. The newer nations of the Third World are similarly being influenced by the forces of secularism, violence and nationalism that are moving throughout East and West and are now affecting South as well as North. This is seen not only in the corruption, graft and greed among many of the leaders in the newer nations leading to constant political revolutions, coups d'état and inter-tribal upheavals and warfare, but also in the suffering of their people through famine, disease and malnutrition. This is something with which we shall deal more fully later.

The writing is on the wall for the nations of the world. Those who have eyes to see and a mind open to the reality of what is happening in the world today can see the warning signs. God is using them to send a message to mankind. Will that message be heard?

PART 3

The Deeds of the Lord

8.

Warning Signs

Isaiah chapter 5 begins with a prophetic song about a vineyard, in which God appeals to the people of Jerusalem to act as his own judge. He presents them with a parable of a vineyard in which the owner clears the ground, plants the choicest vines and does everything possible to tend and care for the vineyard. But when he comes to look for a crop of good grapes it yields only bad fruit. He says, "What more could have been done for my vineyard than I have done for it?"

The conclusion of the parable in the song shows what God will do with his vineyard. He says, "I will take away its hedge, and it will be destroyed; I will break down its wall, and it will be trampled."

Through this prophetic song God sent a very clear warning to the people of Jerusalem that he would withdraw his covering of protection from them and allow them to be exposed to their enemies. He spelled out in the clearest possible terms the interpretation of the parable:

> The vineyard of the Lord Almighty is the house of Israel, and the men of Judah are the garden of his delight.
> And he looked for justice, but saw bloodshed; for righteousness, but heard cries of distress (Isaiah 5:7).

In verse 16 of this same chapter Isaiah makes a theological statement of the greatest significance for an understanding of the nature of God. The statement is this:

But the Lord Almighty will be exalted by his justice, and the Holy God will show himself holy by his righteousness.

It is unfortunate that the NIV translators have somewhat obscured the full impact of this passage by their use of "righteousness" instead of the word "justice", which is a literal translation of the Hebrew word *sadaq*. *Sadaq* is used twice in this sentence; the NIV translates it in the first instance "justice" and the second time as "righteousness". This is no doubt to bring it into line with the common Western concept. The Hebrews thought of justice in terms of *relationships*, whereas the Western understanding, which stems from the culture of the Roman Empire, is a *legalistic* one. To the Hebrew a just man was one who stood in right relationships with God and with his neighbours. To the Western mind, justice is getting one's deserts according to a strict legal code, and righteousness consists of acting in accordance with that same code. Thus in the Western culture right relationships, which are the basis of the Hebrew concept of justice, become lost in a preoccupation with individual behaviour.

Rightly translated this verse should read, "But the Lord Almighty will be exalted by his justice, and the Holy God will show himself holy by his *justice!*" The holiness of God would be shown *by his justice* , and his justice would be seen in his *withdrawing his covering of protection* from Jerusalem and the people of Judah, thus leaving them exposed to their enemies. This would be an act of justice on God's part because he had given warning after warning to the house of Israel and the men of Judah: "He looked for justice, but saw bloodshed." He was looking for right relationships but all he saw was injustice and oppression, murder and violence. What he heard were the cries of distress from the poor and the oppressed. So he gave yet another warning to the rich and the powerful:

Woe to you who add house to house and join field to field
till no space is left and you live alone in the land.

The Lord Almighty has declared in my hearing: "Surely
the great houses will become desolate, the fine mansions
left without occupants" (Isaiah 5:8 and 9).

Isaiah was showing that the very nature of the holiness of God
demands that he cannot continue to protect those who live in
flagrant disobedience to his law, who flout every warning that
he sends to them, and who deliberately rebel against the truth
of his word, thereby breaking the covenant relationship that
exists with him and that he himself has established and
sanctified. God would not be just if he ignored the actions of
such men. He would be denying his very nature if he did
nothing. By removing his protection and allowing his own
beloved people to be overcome by their enemies, and even to
be taken into exile, God would, in fact, be exalting his justice,
upholding his holiness and showing that he himself remains
true to the standard of right relationships that he expects
from his people.

But God never withdraws his protection from his people
without sending them clear warnings. This is what he did in
the time of Isaiah. It was the prophet's task to interpret the
signs of the times to the understanding of the people. Amos
faithfully carried out his task in the northern kingdom of
Israel, and Isaiah did the same for the southerners in Judah
and Jerusalem.

The prophets not only spoke the word of the Lord as it was
revealed to them, but interpreted what God was *actually doing*
in contemporary events in the life of the nation. God thus
spoke very clearly *by word and deed.* He always confirms the
revealed word through his own deeds. The prophets themselves often used this same method by presenting the people
with enacted parables, through which they demonstrated the
word that they were speaking – as when Jeremiah went about

the streets of Jerusalem with a wooden yoke on his shoulders to show how the yoke of Babylon would be put upon the people (Jeremiah 27:2).

God used many ways to speak to his people through what the prophets called the "deeds of the Lord" – including famine, drought, crop disease, economic difficulties and social problems.

Despite many warning signs that were clearly interpreted by the prophet, Isaiah could find no response in the people. He complained:

> But they have no regard for the deeds of the Lord, no respect for the work of his hands.
>
> Therefore my people will go into exile for lack of understanding; their men of rank will die of hunger and their masses will be parched with thirst.
>
> Therefore the grave enlarges its appetite and opens its mouth without limit; into it will descend their nobles and masses with all their brawlers and revellers.
>
> Both low and high will be humbled, and the eyes of the arrogant brought low (Isaiah 5:12-15).

Then there follows the statement that, through these terrible disasters that will come upon the people of Jerusalem and Judah, the holiness and justice of God will be revealed. Thus, far from God being seen as powerless, as one who was unable to protect his people against the onslaught of their enemies, God would be exalted by his justice. He had warned his people clearly, pleading with them to turn away from their sinful ways and re-establish right relationships with himself and within the life of the nation; those pleadings and warnings having been ignored, God's action is to allow his people to suffer and thereby to cleanse an unholy people who have become abhorrent to him.

This message is of the utmost significance for the nations

of the world today. It is vitally important that this basic theological principle should be understood – that God is holy, his very nature is just, and his justice and holiness demand that he only gives full protection to those who are in a right relationship with himself.

Additionally, the very nature of God is love. Jesus revealed this more than any of the prophets, although it was implicit in their message. Because of his great love for his people, especially those who have entered into a right relationship with him through his beloved Son Jesus, God takes the strongest possible steps to warn his people of impending danger. There are certain periods in history which represent greater danger than others. During these periods, when nations are warring against one another, there is a special need for the people of God to be obedient to his word, to be a people who trust him completely and to be responsive to what he is saying to them.

The nature of God is unchanged, for the Bible reveals him as the Eternal God who is the same yesterday, today and for ever. God speaks to us today through his revealed word in Scripture, and through the Holy Spirit whom Jesus promised to all believers. Jesus said, "When he, the spirit of truth, comes, he will guide you into all truth. He will not speak on his own; he will speak only what he hears, and he will tell you what is yet to come" (John 16:13).

It is the solemn promise of Jesus that in times of crisis, when it is necessary for the people of God to have insight into future events, through the ministry of the Holy Spirit among them he will give such prophetic insight. A part of that prophetic insight which God gives is an understanding of the signs of the times and an interpretation of contemporary events in their spiritual significance. This is part of the ministry of the Holy Spirit and is available to the people of God; it becomes of vital significance in times of international crisis, such as the days in which we are now living.

God is sending clear warnings to the nations of the world; it is necessary for the Church to act as prophet to the nations by proclaiming the word of God with power and authority, and by interpreting the deeds of the Lord in such a way that they can be understood even by the secular community. Indeed, the deeds of the Lord are a powerful means of communicating the word of God to the darkened minds of secular men, who are being driven by the forces of destruction that are at large in the world today.

Even secular men can see what is happening in the world. They are affected by these events, and they experience a sense of powerlessness in the face of natural disaster. They realize their vulnerability; even the humanists, who trust only in human ability to solve all the problems that beset mankind, are powerless in the face of natural disaster and the forces that are gaining momentum today. This gives the opportunity to the people of God to act prophetically; they can present the right interpretation of these signs, in the same way as Joseph acted as interpreter to Pharaoh, Jonah to Nineveh and Daniel to Nebuchadnezzar.

The people of God are to be the interpreters of the deeds of the Lord to the people of the world. Once they themselves have a clear understanding of the significance of contemporary events they will be encouraged to speak fearlessly, and will be anointed with power to proclaim the word of God from the housetops.

The economic recession that has hit the world today is one of the signs of the times. Even the finest brains among our economists are unable to control the plight of the world's economy and the increasing confusion of the world's monetary system. The debt mountain of the Third World, which increases month by month and year by year, is already reaching crisis point in a number of these nations, where their gross national product is less than the annual sum required to service their debts – the amount of interest a nation may have to pay on loans from Western bankers is more than the entire income it derives from its exports. In order to stop these nations defaulting on their debts, the bankers simply give them another loan to enable them to pay the interest, and thus the mountain of debt grows higher and becomes more and more impossible to repay. The day when the whole ridiculous system collapses cannot be far delayed. Usury, which is roundly condemned in the Bible, is the basis of this system, and it is inevitable that judgement will fall upon those who so flagrantly flout the word of the Lord.

Family breakdown is another warning sign today. The family, which is the core unit in society, is weaker than ever before in the history of mankind, in most Western nations and is increasingly so, due to urbanization, in many Third World nations. Infidelity, divorce and lack of discipline among children and young people emphasize the disarray and disorder that lie at the heart of society.

Violence in society, social unrest, murder, rape, riots and terrorism are everyday events in most parts of the world today. The incidence of international terrorism, such as the hi-jacking of aeroplanes, hits the world headlines and makes superstars out of the men of violence. This is a day of violence and aggression, when men worship these things and believe that any means are justified by the end. These acts of violence and lawlessness are a clear sign of mankind's rebellion against God.

The number of human disasters that occur today through air crashes, through road and rail accidents, are a further indication of the disorder among the nations. Although these disasters are often due to human error as much as to the deliberate acts of saboteurs and terrorist bombers, they indicate a lack of dedicated care and concern for safety and well-being. This is a sure sign of malaise among the nations. Aircraft may be kept flying in order to produce maximum profits, when they should be stripped down and overhauled.

91

Cars and coaches and even trains are sometimes driven too fast, and carelessly handled by those who care little for the sanctity of life.

Incurable diseases are being used by God himself to add to the signs of the times. He allows things to happen through the natural order that should bring sharp warnings to mankind – certainly to those who have ears to hear and eyes to see and a mind open to God. The many diseases afflicting mankind today are the scourge of millions – cancer, venereal diseases and more recently AIDS, that began among the homosexual communities in the West and is now spreading rapidly among other sections of the population.

Natural disasters due to weather disturbances, crop failure and vegetation disease are resulting in the worst famines known to mankind since the beginning of recorded history. Millions are now dying every year through malnutrition, disease and starvation, in a world where natural resources should be able to provide sufficient for all. But the natural resources are themselves in decline. Men are greedily using up the world's precious oil supply, and squandering irreplaceable minerals through the insatiable avarice of industrial societies and the voracious lust for bigger and bigger profits.

God is clearly warning us of the consequences of our actions. Natural disasters occur with ever greater frequency. There have been more earthquakes this century than at any time since the beginning of recorded history. But still the nations do not hear the word of the Lord or heed his warning signs. The deeds of the Lord are ignored.

Events in South Africa are God's warning to the nations of the world. In 1980 God spoke to me about coming events in South Africa. He showed me that the time was coming when there would be a great uprising among the black peoples of South Africa. He said this would be as a direct result of the injustice of the white minority, who were not acting rightly towards their black neighbours. At the time of writing this book the great upheaval the Lord showed me among the black people has not yet occurred, but I believe it to be very near. In August 1985 I sent to the Prime Minister and Government of South Africa the word that the Lord had given me five years earlier, and which he had told me to guard carefully until the time when it should be released, when I saw the signs begin to happen. The word I sent them was a warning from the Lord that may be the last opportunity to repent. It was a warning to the Government of South Africa and the white minority population to repent before the Lord and seek right relationships with their black neighbours – or the events God had shown to me would take place.

The crisis in South Africa will be seen to be the trigger for a number of other events throughout the world, beginning with the world's monetary system and economic problems. Of even greater significance, the events in South Africa are to serve as a warning to the nations of the West to turn to God and listen to the word of the Lord before it is too late.

*

When will you listen? says the Lord to the nations of the West. O my people, heed my warnings. See the signs I send to you and the things I allow to happen. See the consequences of your own actions. You have rejected my law. You have spurned my word and there is no health in you. That is why there is such sickness and suffering among you. You are like a diseased body full of sores, and yet you will not heed my word. I plead with you to turn to me and believe. Humble yourselves before me and I will be gracious unto you. I will forgive you and heal you. For I, the Lord your God, am a gracious God. I love my children and freely forgive those who turn to me. I reaffirm my promise, that is to all who love me and believe in my beloved Son Jesus. "If my people who are called by my name will humble themselves and pray and turn away from their wicked ways and seek my face I will hear their prayer, I will forgive their sin and I will heal their land."

9.

Revival

The deeds of the Lord are not only to be seen in the warning signs given to mankind but also in the creative activity of the Holy Spirit that is to be found at work among us. There is massive evidence of a fresh move of God which can be seen in many nations. This fresh move of God we may term the acts of God's blessing upon his people; they are in contrast to the warning signs that he sends to call people to change their ways. All the deeds of the Lord are, of course, acts of love, for he cannot act in any other way and be true to himself.

God's nature is merciful, his desire is to include all mankind in the family of those who know him and who stand in a right relationship with him, and his plans for his people are good. God's promises, which Jeremiah sent to the exiles in Babylon are, through the life, death and resurrection of Jesus, extended to all mankind: "For I know the plans I have for you," declares the Lord, "plans to prosper you and not to harm you, plans to give you hope and a future"(Jeremiah 29:11).

In order for God to work out his good plans, the Gospel has to reach all nations and all communities. Jesus said that this would happen before the end of this age. He said, "And this Gospel of the Kingdom will be preached in the whole world as a testimony to all nations, and then the end will come" (Matthew 24:14).

The evidence is mounting worldwide that the fulfilment of this prophecy from Jesus is near and may actually be witnessed in our generation. The Bible Societies estimate that at the present rate of expansion of evangelism and translation of the Bible on every continent, 95 per cent of the world's total population will have been reached with the Gospel, or have access to the Gospel in their own tongue, by the end of this century. This means that by the year AD 2000 every tribe and every community will have the opportunity of hearing the Gospel in their own language or dialect and will thus have the opportunity of receiving Jesus Christ as Lord and Saviour.

This does not mean that the whole population of the world will respond and become believers. The words of Jesus do not envisage that. Even those who heard the Gospel from his own lips during his ministry did not all respond. Indeed vast numbers, including the rulers of the nation, rejected the testimony to the Father and the word of life that he brought. Thus Jesus did not prophesy that a time would come, before the end of the age, when everyone in the total population of the world would be a believer. What he did say was that the Gospel of the Kingdom would be preached in the whole world *as a testimony* to all nations, so that all people of all nations would have the opportunity of choosing eternal life through Christ or of rejecting him.

The history of the expansion of Christianity since the first century AD shows us that the Gospel has gone out among the nations in surges rather than in a uniform pattern of expansion. There have been periods of rapid expansion and there have also been periods of falling away from the faith. The significant thing about the pattern of expansion that has emerged over nearly twenty centuries is that each period of expansion reaches a new high level. It is like the incoming tide, where each fresh wave breaks fresh ground and reaches a new high-water mark. So the incoming tide of the expansion of the Gospel among all nations has gradually surged forward with each new period of expansion, to reach a greater proportion of the world's population.

Today we are witnessing the greatest period of expansion in the history of Christianity. There are many indications that this may be the last such period before the fulfilment of the promises that Jesus gave to his disciples. The plain facts are that more than a quarter of the world's entire population now claim the name of Jesus. This does not mean that all of them have had the same conversion experience, or that there is no nominality among them. It does not mean that all share the same doctrine, worship or even understanding of the Lordship of Jesus. It does not even mean that all will have had the Gospel presented to them in the same way, but it does mean that more than a quarter of the world's total population have heard the name of Jesus and made some kind of positive response to him.

There are a number of factors of particular interest concerning the present period of expansion of the Gospel throughout the world. We need to look carefully at these in order to understand the significance of what God is doing today.

1. **Most rapid**. The present period of expansion of the Gospel is the most rapid since the first century AD and the times of the New Testament Church when the Apostles and the first generation of believers beyond them were carrying the Gospel with power and enthusiasm to all the nations in the known world. The rate of expansion of evangelism and of the response to the Gospel has been increasing since the middle of this century, and the *rate of expansion* is still increasing.

By 1979 the net growth of committed Christians reached 63,000 per day. The information obtainable from churches in many lands, and from missionary societies, evangelistic organizations and individual missionaries, evangelists, preachers and pastors indicated that by 1985 the daily growth rate of new Christians had reached 85,000. In that same year the number of new churches being formed worldwide each week reached 2,500.

The most significant factor was that the rate of expansion

was still increasing, and in some regions the conversion rate exceeded the birth rate. This remarkable factor is to be seen in the continent of Africa. Throughout southern and central Africa – that is, in the whole of Africa south of the Sahara – in almost every country evangelism is bearing fruit at an incredible rate. By 1978 the new-birth rate had overtaken the natural birth rate, and more than six million Christians were being added to the Church every year. This astounding fact means that if the present rate of expansion continues, the day is theoretically in sight when the whole population of central and southern Africa will have accepted Jesus as Lord.

2. **Radical change**. The second remarkable feature of the present period of expansion of the Gospel worldwide is that it is not occurring through what the Church Growth experts call "biological growth" but through conversion experience. In other words, it is not taking place through natural growth due to children being born into Christian families and being nurtured in the faith, but through those who have had little or no previous contact with the Gospel hearing and receiving the word of God and trusting Jesus as their personal Lord and Saviour.

The radical nature of the Gospel being presented and the change that it is bringing in the lives of individuals and whole communities, and sometimes whole nations, is largely due to the nature of the evangelism taking place. It is resulting in an enthusiasm for Christ, and in such an excitement and zeal among new believers that they are powerful witnesses within their own families and communities.

In many areas the expansion of the Gospel is spreading like a prairie fire; it is this spontaneity that is one of the major marks of a new movement of God. Revival is not the work of man or the result of planned evangelism, it is the spontaneous combustion generated by a fresh outpouring of the Holy Spirit upon a people prepared by his own hand.

3. **Indigenous movement**. The spontaneity and enthusiasm of new believers which results in the Gospel spreading rapidly among tribes and communities, and in towns and cities, in many regions is producing an indigenous movement. That is, it is not being led by foreign missionaries but by local people in each area. It is largely the new believers themselves who are witnessing within their own families and communities, and it is from among them that the preachers are being generated who have the anointing of the Spirit of God upon them to reach their own peoples. Thus the Gospel is being preached in many cultures as well as in many major languages and dialects.

When the Gospel is presented in the local culture of a people previously unreached, it comes with a power and impact that is not usually present when it comes from a foreign missionary. He inevitably presents the Gospel through his own understanding and in the context of his own culture, which often has an alien aspect to the hearers.

The indigenous nature of the present period of evangelism in many nations is resulting in a refining of the culture of their people that could never have taken place if the Gospel had been received outside their own cultural context.

4. **Church planting**. The indigenous character of the present period of evangelism is resulting in a great surge in church planting in many countries. These churches are usually established within the *local* culture of a *local* community with *local* leadership. They are the result of the preaching of evangelists from within the local area or region, so that the churches being planted are not linked to missionary organizations in the West or to any of the older orthodox churches or denominations.

This is part of the new character of the present period of church expansion that is unlike that of previous periods. It is not the main-line, traditional churches who are reaching out through missionaries as in previous periods of expansion of the Gospel; God is raising up evangelists and pastors from among the newly reached peoples to enable them to reach their own communities.

Sometimes it is the people of the least social status whom God is using as, for example, in Malaysia where the revival that is beginning to sweep through the urban populations of that nation actually began among the local Malay tribes, most of whom are illiterate. These indigenous peoples, the Muruts, the Lumbawangs, the Kadazaans and the Ibans, mostly live in the coastal villages or the East Malaysian jungle. It is known that revival started there around 1970, but nobody knows how it happened or who was responsible for first taking the Gospel to these people. What is known, however, is that for the past fifteen years or more the Holy Spirit has been sweeping like a consuming fire among these people; all that is now happening among the urban population is really due to their faithfulness.

God is thus using a people who were no people to release another people. The population of urban Malaysia, which is largely made up of incomers from India, China and many other parts of South East Asia and is officially an Islamic stronghold, is being transformed into a Spirit-filled nation of committed Christians. The remarkable feature of the revival taking place there is that the simple tribal peoples, who were the original inhabitants, have been moved by God to pray for the conversion of those who have come in from other lands and who now rule their country.

5. **Signs and wonders**. One of the remarkable features of the present period of rapid expansion of Christianity throughout the world is the accompanying signs and wonders that Jesus said would follow the preaching of the Gospel. These are particularly to be seen among the nations of what we know as the Third World. It is here that faith is at its height, where people from non-sophisticated socio-cultural backgrounds have not had their minds polluted by the

onslaught of secularism which has hit the Western nations during the twentieth century. When they come into faith in the Lord Jesus through the impact of the Gospel, presented by preachers from their own regions and communities who are on fire for the Lord, faith reaches tremendous heights.

It is in such an atmosphere of faith that the Spirit of God is able to minister among the people through mighty miracles. Multitudes of illustrations of the most remarkable miracles could be given; here we have space for only one account. This is taken, not from the records of a Christian preacher, but from the eye-witness account of a secular newspaper reporter and printed, not in a Christian magazine, but in an ordinary daily newspaper – the *Evening Sketch* published in Lagos, Nigeria. It described an evangelistic meeting attended by a crowd reported to be in the region of half-a-million people at the Olabadun Stadium in Ibadan, Nigeria. The preacher was the locally born Nigerian evangelist, Benson Idahosa.

Archbishop Idahosa had not even started to pray when the power of the Almighty descended on the over-crowded stadium. He was still speaking from the Gospel of Luke about Jesus catching the anger of the scribes and pharisees when a thunderous "hallelujah" tore the air from a section of the stadium. Archbishop Idahosa quickly said, "A miracle has happened there." And that is how avalanches of wonders started rolling through the night, left, centre and everywhere in the stadium. There were wonders un-limited, miracles unimaginable.

I saw vividly two women regain their sight; four para-lysed boys walk; two deaf mutes heard and began speaking; a teenage girl struck down by paralysis over nine years ago walked. There were hundreds of other miracles but be-cause of the packed crowds those healed could not mount the rostrum to give their testimony.

One woman who regained her sight said she had been

blind for more than ten years. When asked to give her name to the *Evening Sketch* she shouted,"My name! My name! What does it matter! I can see you now! You are holding a camera. You are wearing a shirt." And that was how it went on far into the night as the power of God came down upon the whole company.

6. **The Third World**. A further remarkable feature about the present period of expansion of the Gospel worldwide is that the most spectacular advances are being made in Third World nations. This is perhaps due to the fact that they have so far been free from the deadening impact of materialism and secularism to the degree that the nations of the Western world have been affected. With multitudes being added to the Lord each year in Africa (six million net growth rate), it is said that Africa is rapidly becoming the new Christian centre of the world.

The faith and enthusiasm of the new Christians in the newer nations is a testimony to the power of the Holy Spirit moving among them; it also serves as a rebuke to the dull traditionalism and nominalism of many Western Christians who have never seen a miracle and don't expect anyone to get converted.

As the expansion rate of the Gospel among Third World nations increases so too does their vision for the Kingdom and their desire to reach others for Christ. Many Christians in these churches in the new nations are beginning to take seriously the great commandment of Jesus to "go into all the world and preach the Gospel to all nations". It is quite possible that very soon they will be sending evangelists to *their* "ends of the earth" which, of course, will be the Western nations.

7. **The Western world**. The Western nations, who have had the Gospel for centuries and who in previous generations have been used by God mightily to take the good news of the

Lord Jesus to many peoples, are not seeing the same spectacular advance of the Gospel as is apparent in Third World nations. Many of the Western nations have grown dull in their faith or have even rejected it through the onslaught of secularism and humanist philosophies. Yet even in these nations there is evidence of a fresh move of God in our generation.

Many churches are being touched by the renewal of the Holy Spirit, giving them a fresh experience of God and a new joy and enthusiasm, both in worship and in sharing their faith with others. There are some nations, such as Finland, where revival has been experienced in recent years, and others, such as Britain, where the renewal movement has been gaining strength, especially among young people, since the early 1970s.

8. **The Eastern nations**. Among the Communist nations of the Eastern world there is also considerable evidence of a fresh move of God. The most spectacular recent evidence of the work of the Holy Spirit in a Communist nation comes from China.

When the Western missionaries were forced to leave China in 1948, following the Communist revolution, there were less than a million Christians in that country with the largest population in the world. Today, now that China is slowly becoming opened up to visitors from the Western world and news of internal events is coming out, the picture of indigenous evangelism that is emerging is an exciting one. From less than a million Christians at the middle of the century, and during a period of severe persecution, the number of committed Christians has multiplied enormously. Some sources put the number of committed Christians today as high as fifty million. It is difficult to get accurate information, and there is an official church which is sanctioned by the Communist authorities, as well as a powerful house church movement. The information being received in the West is by

103

no means clear, so that the picture of what is actually happening in China may not be known for some time. What is absolutely plain is that during a time of persecution of Christians the number of believers has increased dramatically, no doubt through the personal testimony of individuals. It would have been impossible for evangelists and pastors to work openly; the faith had to be shared secretly as an underground movement. But during that time the number of believers multiplied, and now that more tolerant days have arrived, and the Gospel of the Kingdom is being openly preached, many communities are receiving Christ in large numbers, and it may well be that the whole of China stands on the edge of revival.

Perhaps within the purposes of God the Communist purge of religion has been used to break, not only the power of the Mandarins, but also the hold of Buddhism, and Taoism and local ancestor religions that had such a powerful grip upon the Chinese people. Today there is a spiritual vacuum across the nation, and many young people in particular have had no religious background or training; this leaves them open to the Gospel when it is presented to them in their own tongue and by members of their own community who are on fire for the Lord Jesus and are being used as his powerful witnesses.

We have no information as to what is happening in Russia today, but God has been speaking to me a number of times recently about revival there. I have no evidence with which to back this up or statistics to offer, but I am sufficiently convinced that I have been hearing rightly from the Lord to make this statement public. I believe that there is strong evidence of revival in many parts of Russia today. I believe that this evidence is being firmly suppressed by the Communist authorities. But I also believe the day will come when we shall hear of whole towns and regions being reached with the Gospel, and of a fresh outpouring of the Spirit of God upon the people of Russia with signs and wonders following; that is already confounding the Communist authorities.

It may be the intention of the Lord to give a revival in Russia to carry out his purpose of worldwide salvation. The Russian people are disillusioned with the failure of Communism to provide them with the promised Utopia two generations after the Bolshevik revolution. It may well be that the Lord is saying to his people in Russia that, after seventy years in Babylon he has heard the cry of his faithful people and is reaching out to save the nation. This spiritual revival, the work of the Holy Spirit in Russia, together with the famine that I believe God will send upon Russia, and the breaking of their economy would change the entire situation in that land.

10.

Spiritual Gifts

The mounting evidence of a fresh move of God in many regions of the world makes exciting reading for Christians, but what does it mean? Surely when God acts in the world there is a purpose behind it. Of course we know that his ultimate intention is that the Gospel of salvation should be heard by people of all nations. But in order rightly to understand the signs of the times in our own generation we need to be aware of any special significance in the way in which God is acting among his people.

We have already noted that the prophets carefully studied the deeds of the Lord both in terms of warning signs and in terms of spiritual activity such as that in Isaiah's day, when the faith of the people grew during the invasion of Judah by the Assyrians. The word of God was heeded widely, and as the people returned to the Lord in trust and obedience revival broke out in Jerusalem. The result was that the armies of Sennacherib were smitten without the army of Judah being required to fight, and the Assyrians retreated from the land. There is an exciting account of this in 2 Chronicles 30-32, which ends with the terse summary of the chronicler:

And the Lord sent an angel, who annihilated all the fighting men and the leaders and officers of the camp of the Assyrian king. So he withdrew to his own land in disgrace. And when he went into the temple of his God, some of his sons cut him down with the sword. So the Lord saved Hezekiah and the people of Jerusalem from the hand of

Sennacherib king of Assyria and from the hand of all others. He took care of them on every side (2 Chronicles 32:21-22).

When God acts among his people he does so decisively, and for those who have spiritual eyes attuned to God through the Holy Spirit the significance of what he is doing is plain to see.

Clearly today there is a fresh distribution of the gifts of the Holy Spirit among believers. This was foreseen by the prophets. Joel, for example, prophesied that the day would come when God would pour out his Spirit upon believers among all the nations; Peter saw the beginning of this on the Day of Pentecost, at the dawn of the age of the Holy Spirit.

If we are right in our interpretation of the signs of the times in our own day, then what we are seeing is a coming towards a climax of that movement of the Holy Spirit that began at Pentecost. Men and women of all nations are not only hearing the Gospel and receiving the news of salvation through Christ with great joy, but are being filled with the power of the Spirit, and are seeing God at work in their lives in ways that surpass human strength and ability.

What we are seeing today is a fresh distribution of the gifts of the Holy Spirit in a manner similar to that which happened in the days of the New Testament Church, when the first believers were rejoicing in the power of the Spirit of God that had come upon them. Their joy and zeal for the Lord, their consciousness of his presence among them, their trust in him and their great faith not only bubbled over in eagerness to share their faith with others and be living witnesses for the Lord Jesus, but also to exercise the various gifts that they found among themselves as members of the body of Christ.

The New Testament, especially in the writings of Paul, gives ample evidence of the exercise of spiritual gifts among ordinary believers, not just among the leadership, the elders and Apostles. Paul, in Ephesians, emphasizes the unity of the

107

body of Christ. He says, "There is one body and one Spirit – just as you were called to one hope when you were called – one Lord, one faith, one baptism; one God and Father of all; who is over all and through all and in all." Paul goes on to emphasize that "to each one of us grace has been given as Christ apportioned it. This is why it says: 'When he ascended on high, he led captives in his train and gave gifts to men'" (Ephesians 4:4-8). These gifts Paul distinguishes as a variety of ministry gifts and a variety of spiritual gifts. Not all believers are appointed with ministry gifts, which carry special responsibilities within the body of Christ, but all are able to receive spiritual gifts and to exercise them within the body.

Paul teaches that the gifts are given for the strengthening and building up of the body of Christ. "From him the whole body, joined and held together by every supporting ligament, grows and builds itself up in love, as each part does its work" (Ephesians 4:16). Thus it is through the exercise of spiritual gifts by every member that the body life of the community of believers is built up. Each one must exercise the gifts given to him by God. Otherwise, if one part of the body is inactive, that part will wither and become unhealthy, and may even communicate disease to other parts of the body.

Indigenization

We have already noted the indigenous nature of the present remarkable period of worldwide expansion of the Gospel, especially in Third World nations. The significance of this is that what is happening in these nations is very clearly a movement of the Holy Spirit *from within*, rather than something that is coming from outside. God is generating new spiritual life from within the nations by a fresh outpouring of his Spirit upon them, and by the anointing of his Spirit upon individuals within those nations. As the Spirit begins to touch the lives of more and more ordinary people within the newer nations, it becomes clearer what God is actually doing. He is raising up the humble poor. He is calling people who were no people to be *his* people. He is doing what Mary the mother of Jesus saw with prophetic insight and sang about in her song of praise to the Lord when she knew she was to be the mother of Christ:

> He has performed mighty deeds with his arm; he has scattered those who are proud in their inmost thoughts. He has brought down rulers from their thrones but has lifted up the humble. He has filled the hungry with good things and sent the rich empty away (Luke 1:51-53).

God is building up a body of people who love him from among the ordinary humble poor of all nations. He long ago established the spiritual principle of the body of Christ, in which there should be no élites but where the greatest should be the servant and the servant should be the greatest. The only status distinctions recognized by God are between believer and unbeliever; between those who have the status of sons of God and those who do not. Indeed there are only two classes of men today – those who belong to Christ and those who belong to the world.

Jesus promised that the Gospel would turn the values of the world upside down and this is the way in which it is happening today. This is true "body ministry", in which each one exercises the gifts given to them. These gifts have different functions but the same status. Thus each member of the body of Christ has the same value in the eyes of God and should be similarly valued by other members of the body. Body life should function without recognition of any differences in *status* but with careful regard to differences of *function* according to the gifts of the Spirit.

Signs and Wonders

The presence of the Spirit of God among believers brings new power into the hands of the servants of God. This power, when rightly exercised under the direction of the Holy Spirit and in the context of faith and trust in the Lord, results in many signs and wonders – events that the world labels "miracles". In the words of Jesus, these are to be expected as the normal everyday occurrences that will accompany the faithful preaching of the Gospel and the love and trust of the people of God.

Jesus promised that believers who are filled with his presence and power through the Holy Spirit would do even greater things than he did. This seems an impossible word, but it is in fact true. It must be true because Jesus said so! But the evidence of its truth is being seen today. Jesus' ministry was bounded by the geographical limitations of his earthly ministry. Today the believers in the Lord Jesus are to be found in every community and every nation, in every region and every continent of the world. Thus the body of Christ is able to do greater things than Jesus did during the time of his ministry in Galilee and Judea. Perhaps this was what he meant.

The gifts of the Holy Spirit that God has given to the believers enable them to minister within the body and also to carry out the work of Christ in the world. Jesus promised that when believers obey his command to carry the Gospel to all nations, they do not go in their own strength, neither do they go alone. The anointing power of the Holy Spirit will be upon them and he will be beside them, within them and surrounding them with his presence, even in times of severe testing, persecution and trouble. Through Isaiah God promised:

Fear not, for I have redeemed you; I have called you by name; you are mine.

When you pass through the waters, I will be with you; and when you pass through the rivers, they will not sweep over you.

110

When you walk through the fire, you will not be burned;
the flames will not set you ablaze. For I am the Lord your
God (Isaiah 43:1-3).
Though the mountains be shaken and the hills be removed, yet my unfailing love for you will not be shaken nor
my covenant of peace be removed, says the Lord, who has
compassion on you (Isaiah 54:10).

Jesus reaffirmed this promise throughout his teaching, and he
concluded his great commission with the promise, "And
surely I will be with you always, to the very end of the age"
(Matthew 28:20).

Each One Reach One

The presence and power of God among the believers results
in every believer being a witness to Christ. This is the intention of God for his people. It is his intention that each one
should reach one, that all believers should be able naturally to
share their faith in Christ with others. A living faith cannot be
confined. It must be communicated to others, within the
family and within the community. Of course, there is often a
cost to this where there is resistance, but the true believers in
the Lord Jesus have a powerful personal experience of Christ,
and have available to them the power of the Holy Spirit within
their lives, so that they cannot keep silent. Even if their words
are muted their lives bear a living testimony to the power of
the Spirit of God within them.

A part of the intention of God for his Church in these
times is to raise "a people of power", where each one knows
him personally, is submitted to him and is able to stand in the
power of the Lord. This is very different from the kind of
community in which only the leaders have power. It is for this
reason that God is giving a fresh distribution of the gifts of
the Spirit such as we are seeing today. The Lord is raising an

army to go against the enemy; it is an army in which each one is able to understand the nature of the warfare and the strategy of God, and to be an active participant in the battle rather than passive cannon fodder.

A lesson from modern warfare may serve to illustrate what is happening and also the strategy of the Lord. With modern tactical nuclear weapons a massed brigade of thousands of soldiers could be wiped out in a few seconds by a single weapon. But where an army is dispersed, as in guerrilla warfare, and where each soldier is trained to stand on his own and not be dependent upon his general for decisions before any action, the army cannot be wiped out by the enemy. He may have limited success in one area or another, but the army fights on.

The nature of the spiritual warfare in which we are engaged today demands that each believer should have some understanding of the battle, as well as a measure of the power of God which will enable him to overcome the wiles of the enemy and to be under the direction of the power of God.

Commitment

It is the measure of the commitment of the believers, rather than their numbers, that indicates strength within the army of the Lord. David had to learn this lesson when he was severely rebuked by God for numbering his army. Through this he was reminded that it was not *his* army, but the Lord's! And he was reminded also of the lesson that God does not save through numbers (1 Chronicle 21).

Gideon similarly had to learn a lesson of absolute trust in the Lord when the 32,000 men of Israel who responded to his call to come and join him in the battle against the Midianites and the Amalekites were whittled down to a mere three hundred. Yet it was through this handful of men that God chose to save the nation. Gideon's army was a highly trained, committed, dedicated, obedient and loyal band of men, who trusted the Lord and were able to be used by him to win a significant battle. This saw the turning of the tide and the saving of Israel from her enemies (Judges 7).

The spiritual lesson to be learned here is that God does not save through numbers but through absolute commitment. He saves through the trust and obedience of his people. In a day when we are rejoicing over the fresh move of God that is bringing multitudes to Christ and adding millions to the Church of God, we must beware of thinking that numbers indicate strength. The mighty miracles God is working among his people are a constant reminder that we can achieve nothing in our own strength. God is giving to us in this generation the same message that he has given to his people many times before, that is "not by might nor by power but by my Spirit, says the Lord Almighty" (Zechariah 4:6).

PART 4

The Church Today

11.

Stumbling Blocks

There are a number of danger signs in the Church today that Christians will do well to note and to heed. In a time when the Spirit of God is moving among most of the nations of the world and bringing millions into the Kingdom every year, the ravenous wolves against which Paul and Jesus warned us are loose among the flock. It seems almost inevitable that when there is a mighty work of God in progress there will be dangers to be faced.

The major danger to which we are drawing attention here is from the impact of the twin forces of secularism and materialism upon the Church and the whole field of Christian mission.

Paul warned the believers in the early Church not to conform to the standards of the world or succumb to its pressures, but to allow their minds to be transformed by the renewing power of the Spirit and the Word of God. He says, "Do not conform any longer to the pattern of this world, but be transformed by the renewing of your mind. Then you will be able to test and approve what God's will is – his good, pleasing and perfect will" (Romans 12:2). J.B. Phillips' translation gets to the heart of what Paul is trying to convey: he says, "Don't let the world around you squeeze you into its own mould, but let God re-mould your minds from within."

This is one of those warnings that Christians have either never fully comprehended or have simply ignored – and never more so than in our own generation. We live in an age when the forces of secularism and materialism are rampant, and are extremely subtle in the manner in which they seep into almost every activity of man.

The Western Church in particular has almost been overcome by the heavy punches of the enemy, using the forces of secularism and materialism. The greatest deception has been in the field of biblical scholarship where, under the guise of the pursuit of truth, there has arisen a generation of liberal secularists who call themselves theologians. The other great deception is that, under the guise of promoting the Gospel and serving the mission of Christ, great materialistic institutions have arisen calling themselves churches and para-church organizations.

The Liberal Secularists

The extent to which the faith of ordinary people in the Western world has been undermined by the teaching of liberal theology is one of the greatest scandals in the entire history of the Church. It is probably unique in the history of any of the world's major religions, that the confidence of believers should actually have been undermined not from outside the faith but from within, by those whose task it is to teach the faith. What is probably also unique is that the attacks upon the veracity and reliability of the Bible have also come from the same source. In no other world religion have the teachers of that religion torn asunder the credibility of their own sacred writings!

All these attacks upon Scripture have been carried out in the cause of the pursuit of truth. Those of a more conservative persuasion have reacted by dismissing or ignoring much of modern scholarship. Thus the great divide has opened up between the so-called liberal theologians and the conservative theologians. This in turn has generated and established the lie that you can either have men of deep spiritual conviction and faith, or scholars, but you cannot have both, because the one contradicts the other.

It is part of the arrogance of the liberal secularists to pose as the only scholars; in this they have been aided and abetted by many conservative thinkers, who are afraid to face some of the knotty problems of authorship and textual criticism for fear of the Bible losing its authority. What they fail to realize is that the word of God does not need the intellect of man to defend it. The word of God is in itself truth; therefore its fundamental nature can neither be altered nor harmed by secularist attacks upon it. It is clearly a mistake for scholars to fall into a blind literalism that defends every word of a rather poor translation into English made more than three hundred years ago, and which has acquired the veneration of age. What they are defending in fact is *antiquity and tradition* rather than the authoritative word of God.

Liberal secularists, on the other hand, begin from a critical position in which debate leads to doubt upon even the most fundamental tenets of the Christian faith. First the Virgin Birth, then the Miracles, then the Resurrection and even the Divinity of Christ have become the subject of speculation and doubt. Following this path there are no certainties left and the Scriptures become reduced to an interesting collection of cultural myths that may be profitably studied more from an anthropological standpoint than from the standpoint of theology, in the search for ultimate truth about God, man and the universe.

In the face of this kind of attack, from men who clearly have no faith in God and are themselves secularists, it is easy to understand the reactions of conservatives in dismissing all modern scholarship and retreating into literalism. Yet it is a gross error to dismiss all modern scholarship. Many of the authorship debates, for example, do not undermine the authority of the word of God. After all, it does not matter at all whether Paul wrote Hebrews, or whether Priscilla wrote it and later generations ascribed it to Paul in order to give it additional authority. You do not need to be a Greek scholar to

119

see that the style of Hebrews is very different from anything else that Paul wrote. The indisputable fact is that whoever wrote Hebrews was inspired by the Spirit of God to bring a message of eternal value to the world.

One of the failings of modern man is our obsession with the personal lives of others. Hence the media's focus upon every detail of the lives of pop personalities and the world's celebrities. In the ancient Hebrew and Greek worlds from which our Bible has come, it was common practice for humble writers to dedicate their work to great men. If it was accepted, it would often be ascribed to the great man and the identity of the humble author would remain obscure. In those days men were more concerned with the message than the messenger. Today we are more concerned with the messenger than the message!

The right starting point for a study of Scripture should be that of personal experience of the Lordship of Jesus and the presence and power of the Holy Spirit, together with a recognition that God has carefully guarded, watched over and preserved the collection of sacred writings we have in our Bible. From the sure and firm foundation of faith in God and a belief in the ultimate authority of the word of God, the most searching scholarship may be pursued without fear. Such scholarship can only lead to a greater revelation of the truth. It certainly will not undermine faith. What we are saying is that it is a false dichotomy to assume that a Christian must either be a person of faith or a scholar. The true dichotomy is between belief and unbelief!

It is a sad fact of history over the past hundred years or more that as secularism has undermined faith in God, secularist scholars have obtained influential positions in the teaching institutions of the Church and universities where ministers and clergy are trained. Under the guise of scholarship, two or three generations of preachers have been subjected to the onslaught of secularists, going like lambs to the slaughter with a simple faith in God only to have it shattered and torn asunder by men of powerful intellect and persuasion. These men are able to use their superior learning to pour scorn on the simple belief and trust of theological students called into ministry, vast numbers of whom have had their confidence in the word of God in the Bible completely destroyed. They have therefore been unable to preach the Gosple with power and conviction, and have gone into the ministry of the Church as little more than well-meaning social workers preaching a weak form of social morality and good citizenship.

The great majority of ministers and clergy in the mainstream churches never see anyone converted throughout their lifetime in ministry, and they never see a miracle. They do not see conversions because they do not preach the Gospel that presents a challenge to the unconverted. They do not see miracles because miracles are the signs and wonders that follow the preaching of the Gospel, and they do not preach the Gospel. In their hearts they know this, so they have no expectations of God doing anything through their ministry. They know this because most of them began with a simple experience of God, and they know they havè lost this experiential foundation of faith; they are powerless to recover it because they are not open to the Holy Spirit.

The tragedy is that these men are the official representatives of God to the world, and they are the shepherds of the sheep in the Church and nation. They are blind guides leading the blind. They are false shepherds misleading the flock. The Church would be far better off without them! They should face up to the fact of their lack of faith and get out of the ministry of the Church. They are a hindrance to the mission of Christ in the world! Alternatively, they should earnestly seek the face of God with weeping and penitence, asking for the Holy Spirit in their lives. The Father, who loves them dearly, and knows the sincerity of their hearts and what has brought them to this point, would embrace them immediately and fill them with his Spirit and the power of his presence. I can testify to this from my own experience, and to the love and mercy of God and all that he can do with one who is steeped in secularist theology and groping through the darkness of loss of faith through intellectual pursuit.

My words are not intended to be hard and judgemental – indeed I do not feel like that towards my brothers in ministry – quite the reverse! I have a deep burden for them. I long for them to know again the joy of salvation we each of us had in the days of our pre-seminary innocence. It is love for them and a deep concern for the work of Christ that causes me to write sternly. We will one day, each of us, be called to account for our ministries – the sacred trust given into our hands by the Lord.

Ezekiel has a stern word to say to shepherds who do not rightly care for the flock:

> You have not strengthened the weak or healed the sick or bound up the injured. You have not brought back the strays or searched for the lost. You have ruled them harshly and brutally. So they were scattered because there was no shepherd, and when they were scattered they became food for all the wild animals . . . .
>
> Because my flock lacks a shepherd and so has been plundered and has become food for all the wild animals, and because my shepherds did not search for my flock but cared for themselves rather than for my flock . . . . I am against the shepherds and will hold them accountable for my flock. I will remove them from tending the flock (Ezekiel 34:4, 5, 8 and 10).

The Evangelical Materialists

Among the many warnings that Paul gave to Christians in the early Church there is none more applicable to us in this materialistic worldly age than the warning he gave to the Christians in Colossae:

> See to it that no one takes you captive through hollow and deceptive philosophy, which depends on human tradition and the basic principles of this world rather than on Christ (Colossians 2:8).

This is a warning that every Christian needs to ponder carefully. We can so easily be taken "captive" through hollow and deceptive beliefs and values that stem from humanism and secularist principles rather than from the Gospel. That is what Paul is saying. He is warning us that it is very easy to be hoodwinked into thinking that we are serving Christ, when in fact we are being driven by the same materialistic and secular forces that are driving the rest of mankind.

This warning is one of the most neglected warnings in the New Testament. Paul reminds the Church that "You have been given fullness in Christ who is the head over every power and authority" (verse 10). So there is no need for any Christian to lack power in facing up to the pressures exerted by this world. There is also no excuse for succumbing to the secular forces that drive Christians into conformity with the world. When this happens it is because we are not claiming the power and the authority of Christ over the principalities and powers, over the spiritual forces of evil that seek to dominate our lives and to take control of the Christian communities and institutions of which we are a part – including our churches.

The great institutions that we call "the Church" today bear little or no resemblance to the Church of the New Testament. They have been subjected to the fiercest onslaughts of the enemy, who uses the subtlest weapons of worldly desires, drives and ambitions that are readily implanted into the minds of men. We can so easily convince ourselves that we are serving God, when we are in fact inflating our own egos, building our own empires and enjoying our own little measures of worldly status and achievement.

Christians in the Bible-believing sector, who have the keenest drives towards evangelization, are the most vulnerable to the spirit of materialism and to doing things in worldly ways, or, in the words of Paul, to using methods that depend upon "the basic principles of this world rather than on Christ". It is too easy to rationalize our own desires; to make plans and ask God to bless them, rather than to seek God's plans and his ways. So many evangelicals have swallowed the lie that "big is beautiful, and bigger is better!" The desire to grow bigger and bigger churches is often from mixed motives and becomes the subject of boasting about numbers rather than about spirituality and effectiveness of witness. In America there is a premier league of big churches, where success is measured by the number of Sunday morning services held to accommodate the congregation. Television and radio ministries that appeal to the multitudes for millions of dollars for their own support have become a materialistic obscenity before God, and do more to bring the Gospel into disrepute and to drive people from Christ than they do to win the world to the Saviour who began as a carpenter in Nazareth.

The great danger of big churches is that they usually do not encourage a whole body of Christ ministry. They produce churches with active pastors and passive people, rather than communities of believers on fire for the Lord, in which every life is committed to sharing the faith and winning others for Christ.

There is a similar danger with crusade evangelism, which so often does little or nothing to strengthen the local church. At best it adds a few more members and at worst it undermines and removes the effectiveness of the local church in evangelism. It does this through creating the myth that the most effective form of evangelism is through the preaching of superstar evangelists, whereas the reverse is true! Among those who are in membership of churches in areas where there have been large evangelistic crusades, only one per cent committed their lives to Christ through crusade evangelism. Eighty per cent made a personal commitment of their lives through the personal witness of other Christians!

Personal witness is the New Testament pattern of evangelism. Every believer was to be a witness, not just those who had special ministry gifts. The true New Testament-type church today is one in which all the committed believers have such a powerful experience of Christ in their own lives that their words and actions act as a powerful witness to the lives of others, so that all who know them are confronted by Christ. Even those who are the least eloquent may be able, through the depths of their sincerity and conviction, to persuade others to accompany them to a church where the Gospel is preached, that they may have the opportunity of accepting Christ for themselves.

The extent to which the modern Church has been moulded by the masters of Mammon is one of the greatest achievements of the enemy today. Many of the large and powerful Christian organizations that have grown up in the second half of this century are a monument to Mammon rather than a source of honour to Christ.

I believe God is saying to us: Listen! You are being hoodwinked and deluded by "hollow and deceptive philosophy, which depends on human tradition and the basic principles of this world rather than on Christ!" Stop looking for methods of evangelism that follow the way of the world and create superstar Christian heroes and superstar aspirants in a day of media madness.

Stop trying to do these things using the ways of the world. Stop taking pride in your great institutions of power and learning. Stop allowing your lives to be dominated by meetings, committees, conferences and all the paraphernalia of human organizations and worldly pursuits.

You are the body of Christ! You are the temple of the Holy Spirit. You are anointed with the power of God. To you he has given gifts. It is to you, the Spirit-filled members of the body of Christ, that he is looking to evangelize the world.

God wants the body of Christ to be an active, Spirit-filled company of believers who understand his great purposes and who are aware of the seriousness of the world situation today; who know that the enemy is waging relentless warfare against mankind and that the only hope lies in the victory of the Lord over the forces of evil.

Christ wants to involve his Church in that battle, that the believers may share with him in the joy of victory; it is for this reason that there is a worldwide fresh outpouring of the Spirit of God today. The Lord is re-arming his Church with the power of his Spirit. He is calling all believers into active service under the banner of the King of Kings.

12.

Clear Discernment

It seems almost too trite to say that we live in a momentous age. World-shattering events are almost everyday occurrences in this generation. They are dramatized and pre-packaged by a highly professional media of international communicators, and transmitted instantly across the nations and into the homes of hundreds of millions of people in almost every region of the world. We become punch-drunk with tragedies, disasters, acts of terrorism, sabotage, earthquakes, famine, disease and human suffering. The media appear to have a preoccupation with the bad news, and all too rarely communicate the multitude of good things happening in the world that are simply not considered newsworthy. We are so bombarded with bad news that it would be understandable if we became reluctant to open our newspapers or switch on the television for fear of what is happening in the world today.

Christians are also aware of the fresh move of God that is taking place in many regions of the world today. The vast increase in the number of committed Christians, the success of evangelism, and enthusiasm for faith sharing, the commitment to prayer and intercession, and the signs and wonders are all indications of the activity of God in our generation and a fresh movement of the Holy Spirit and the presence of the Lord in his Church.

Even non-Christians are aware that these are significant days in the history of the world. It is therefore understandable that Bible-believing Christians should be turning to the

Scriptures more and more to study the word of God and to try to understand the spiritual significance of events in our day. This is both right and proper; it also has its dangers. This is a day when there is an urgent need for clear discernment so that the people of God are not misled by half-truths, wrong emphases and false interpretations. If the believers do not have clear discernment there is likely to be confusion and disunity within the Church. Furthermore, the Church as the body of Christ will be unable to carry out the work of Christ in the most critical period of history for two thousand years. There will be a lack of a clear proclamation of the word of God to the nations. As Paul puts it, "If the trumpet gives an unclear sound who will prepare himself for battle?" (Corinthians 14:8).

There is an urgent need for a simple and clear declaration of the word of God for our times. This can only come from God himself. It is inevitable that in such a day as ours there will be false teaching, but God has given us the means of discerning the truth through the Bible and the Holy Spirit.

Human intellect alone will mislead us, as we become driven by all the forces of humanistic secularism. But to neglect intellect is to cut ourselves off from one of God's most precious gifts to his children. It is absolutely essential that our intellects should be refined, guided and directed by the infilling of the Spirit of the living God. It is the Spirit-filled intellect that is able to perceive the truth in Scripture that God is highlighting in our day; it is the Spirit-filled intellect that is able to weigh and discern the true revelation of God that comes directly to man. Paul was a man of powerful intellect but until he received the Holy Spirit that changed his life and brought him under the discipline and direction of the Lord he was not serving God; he was rather serving the traditions of men.

I do not wish to be negative in this chapter, neither do I wish to sound harshly critical of brothers and sisters in the

Lord who are sincere believers but whom I nevertheless believe to be sincerely mistaken in some of the emphases of their teaching. I do not claim a monopoly of the truth – indeed I am constantly aware of the dangers and pitfalls of the prophetic ministry, and of the need for careful testing and clear discernment of the word of God. It is *his word*, not ours, and therefore it is a sacred obligation upon us to discern rightly what God is saying before we make any pronouncement in his name.

The fear of getting it wrong and the burden of getting it right are constantly with me. Indeed, it is a burden that never leaves me day or night. The awesomeness of the prophetic task is that a man – a mere human being like other men – is called to be a mouthpiece of God. He knows that the day will come when he will have to face the most Holy and Almighty God, Creator of the ends of the earth, sustainer of the universe, and he will have to give an account of his ministry. The man carrying such a prophetic burden is only sustained by his knowledge that this same Almighty God is the Father of our Lord and Saviour Jesus Christ, whom Jesus taught us to call Abba, Father.

I emphasize again that I do not have a monopoly of the truth, but I know that the Holy Spirit within gives me a spirit of disquiet when I hear teaching that is not right or has a wrong emphasis or is likely to mislead others. I have learned to be sensitive to that disquietness, as well as to the warm response or the leap within my spirit at the voice of my Lord – in much the same way as Elizabeth acknowledged that the unborn baby John-the-Baptist leapt in the womb at the presence of the Lord Jesus when Mary came to greet her. I cannot explain these things and I do not intend to try to do so. They are the workings of the Holy Spirit that take many years to learn to distinguish rightly. Even then the rational processes of our intellectual minds are unable to provide formulae to account for them or to teach others. These are

129

things that each of us must learn for ourselves through prayer, meditation, study of the word and humbly standing in the counsel of the Lord.

I have said all these things in the introduction to this chapter to provide the right context for sounding warnings concerning some of the teachings that are popular among quite large sections of Christians today. I do so, from the most urgent desire to see Christians rightly discerning the signs of the times, understanding the great and good purposes of our God, and knowing clearly what he is saying to us today so that the Church may be in right order to meet the immense challenge of the forces of darkness that are gathering momentum in the world. Only thus may the body of Christ be fully mobilized and armed for the battle, having clear discernment, and strengthened with might through the power of the Holy Spirit so that we may be as a mighty army endued with wisdom from on high, directed by the presence of the Lord in our midst and moving towards the ultimate and assured victory that is his.

My deep concern is with the misuse of Scripture through half-truths and wrong emphases. As a general principle we need constantly to bear in mind that truth taken out of context and over-emphasized in isolation from the whole word of God becomes error.

Dates and Times

I am deeply concerned about the many predictions of dates and times that are current among Christians today. I believe that to offer such predictions is contrary to the teaching of Jesus. Jesus said, "It is not for you to know the times or dates the Father has set by his own authority" (Acts 1:7). He was directly rebuking his own disciples who were enquiring about the time when God would restore sovereign independence to the nation Israel.

It is perfectly true that Jesus promised that the Holy Spirit would reveal the future (John 16:13), but this is not to satisfy our mere human curiosity. The unbelievers go to fortune tellers, study the stars, consult spiritist mediums and occultists in a vain desire to know the future. Christians who indulge in Bible mathematics, producing complicated charts and timetables to work out their theories and offering their predictions are misusing the Bible out of vain curiosity; they are in grave danger of coming under the same condemnation as the unbelievers.

Jesus said we are to be a "watching and praying people" who are *always* prepared for his coming, who are living in daily expectation of God speaking to them and working through their lives, and of God at work in his Church and among the nations of the world. He did not promise that we should know the date of his return; he said that we should use our Spirit-filled intellects to understand the signs of the times, that we may rightly interpret the word of God to others in our generation. Jesus spoke sternly to the pharisees who could interpret the signs in the physical world by looking into the sky, seeing the clouds and predicting rain. But they were unable to discern the spiritual signs of the times (Luke 12:54-56).

The Rapture

Those who have a preoccupation with the Rapture, the taking of believers up into heaven, are in grave danger of failing to carry out the work of Christ in the world today. I personally do not believe that the Church will be spared going through at least some of the events that the Bible describes as the Great Tribulation. This would be against the whole witness of Scripture and the ways of the God, who so loved the world as to send his only begotten Son, and who did not spare him but delivered him up for us all, to suffer death on the cross.

131

I believe God will carry the Church *through* at least some of the days of great tribulation that are coming upon the world. He will never leave or forsake those who put their trust in him, and he will bring them through to glorious victory. Whatever interpretation is right is really irrelevant, and probably none of us will have the opportunity in this life of saying, "I told you so!" But the really important issue is that we should be a people who are rightly proclaiming the word of God for our times. We cannot do this effectively if we have a conviction that we are part of an élite group whom God will remove from this earth before he sweeps down in punitive judgement to annihilate all those who don't hold the same views as we do. It doesn't really matter who is right and who is wrong in this eschatological timing. But it does matter supremely that we do not neglect the urgent task that God has given us in the here and now.

The Mark of the Beast

The preoccupation with eschatological theories is leading many Christians into a bondage of fear. There is a kind of superstition surrounding the numbers 666, and some Christians are even afraid to have this sequence in their telephone number! There are a number of popular books, magazines and tapes widely circulating among Christians that are misleading many with their false teaching. The fundamental error is to fail to distinguish between symbol and reality. This is where it is essential for Christians to exercise their intellects under the wisdom and direction of the Holy Spirit. There is the greatest danger in enthusiastic Christians with no theological training or scholarship, knowing nothing of the difference between apocalypse and straight prophecy, offering literalist interpretations of biblical symbolism, and building upon them all kinds of strange theories that link in with their own inadequate understanding of the economic and social forces of change in the modern world.

There are even new Christians whose imaginations have been excited by these theories, and who are posing as teachers of the word and misleading many. They are blind guides misleading the blind! Of course there is some truth in the advancing forces of economic and social decay whose objective is the enslavement of mankind, but to equate this with the issue of numbers on credit cards, and to link the mark of the beast with some form of identification that prevents the fraudulent use of other people's bank accounts, is sheer and utter nonsense. The mark of the beast is a *spiritual* mark and needs a spiritual interpretation.

Shepherding

This is a day of great spiritual activity, when God clearly is at work among his people. In all such times when there is an awareness of the critical days in which we live, Christians become impatient to be moving on at a faster pace, in worship, in the exercise of spiritual gifts, in evangelism, in renewing the structures or reorganizing church life, in changing lifestyles, in programmes of caring, and in many other aspects of Christian life and witness. In such a day it is inevitable that division will arise due to frustration and impatience, as well as to genuine spiritual creativity under the direction of the Spirit of God. We have already noted that new churches are being planted at the rate of two thousand five hundred a week. No doubt this does not include the many little breakaway fellowships and house church groups that result from disagreements within existing churches.

In such a time of spiritual creativity and new activity as we have today, it is inevitable that wrong emphases containing some truth will be popularized and propagated widely. These usually contain an element of biblical truth but are divorced from the whole truth. There are numerous examples today such as "Shepherding", which emphasizes the need for sub-

133

mission, but is usually interpreted as submission to one or two men. The Bible teaching is that we submit to Christ and to each other within the body of Christ. There are many fellowships today that are so bound under the authoritarian domination of a small group of leaders that they are unable to think for themselves, to form sound judgements in their own lives under the direction of the Spirit of God, or to exercise the spiritual gifts that they have been given. Such authoritarian leadership does nothing to build up the body of Christ; it only spiritually numbs the members and reduces them to pew fodder, in much the same way as the priest- and clergy-ridden traditional churches from which many of these same people have turned away to seek true spiritual freedom! They have simply exchanged one form of bondage for another.

Prosperity Cults

Another highly popular false teaching today is that of the "prosperity" people who teach "God wants you rich". What an utter reversal of the teaching of Jesus this is! How can men who claim to be Bible-believers so stand on end the teaching of Jesus! There is not one word in the New Testament that could support such teaching. It is based upon the ancient Hebrew understanding of prosperity in material terms, which was equated with the blessing of God. Job had to learn the falsity of this. The prophets denounced it, and the teaching of Jesus demolished it. But there are Christian so-called teachers today who are trying to revive these ancient heresies! They are driven by the spirit of materialism of this age.

Jesus did not say, "God wants you rich". He said, "Woe to you who are rich, for you have already received your comfort. Woe to you who are well-fed now, for you will go hungry!" (Luke 6:24 and 25). Jesus did not say, "Blessed are you rich for you possess the blessing of God". He said the opposite:

"Blessed are you who are *poor*, for yours is the kingdom of God" (Luke 6:20).

Thus says the Lord to those false teachers who are deluding the people of God in the prosperity cults in the Church today:

> Now listen, you rich people, weep and wail because of the misery that is coming upon you. Your wealth has rotted, and moths have eaten your clothes. Your gold and silver are corroded. Their corrosion will testify against you and eat your flesh like fire. You have hoarded wealth in the last days (James 5:1-3).

One of the saddest features of the modern Church is the way in which the twin spirits of secularism and materialism have infiltrated among the believers. It is too easy to justify our large institutions, our big organizations and even our amassed wealth, on the grounds that it is all needed in order to carry out the mission of Christ in the world today. The Greek Orthodox Church, the Church of Rome, the Church of England, the Lutheran Church and many of the great denominations are immensely wealthy.

Who told the Church of Rome to acquire its fabulous riches? Who told the Church of England to become the greatest land- and property-owning institution in Britain? Who told the Western Protestant churches to build up huge portfolios of investments rivalling those of the great multinational corporations in the empires of Mammon? Who told the pastors, priests and ministers to seek the best livings in the opulent suburbs or city centre parishes, while the run-down inner-city pastorates among the urban poor, the immigrant and the under-privileged are neglected? The extent to which materialism has moulded the mission of the modern Church, to make it unrecognizable in comparison with the Church of the New Testament, needs to be a matter of the

135

most urgent repentance if the Lord is to be able to use the Church as his body in the world at such a time as this.

Division

Over and beyond the worldliness, materialism and secularism that has crept into the Church today, by far the greatest offences before the Lord among the people of God are the divisions and lack of love among us. The great divides between Conservative and Liberal, between Catholic and Protestant, between charismatic and evangelical, between traditional and progressive; between denominations, fellowships, organizations and institutions; between Pentecostal and non-Pentecostal, house church and mainstream church, Eastern and Western, orthodox and non-orthodox, and the multitude of other divisions among us – these are the nails in the hands and feet of the Lord and the thorns that press into his brow. We are crucifying Christ afresh with our lack of love, with our divisions, with our competitiveness, with our bigotry and with our failure to walk humbly and simply before the Lord, in honour preferring one another and building one another up.

James spoke sternly to the Christians in his day:

> You adulterous people, don't you know that friendship with the world is hatred towards God? Anyone who chooses to be a friend of the world becomes an enemy of God. Or do you think Scripture says without reason that the spirit he caused to live in us tends towards envy, but he gives us more grace? That is why Scripture says: "God opposes the proud but gives grace to the humble."
>
> Submit yourselves, then, to God. Resist the devil, and he will flee from you. Come near to God, and he will come near to you. Wash your hands you sinners, and purify your hearts, you double-minded. Humble yourselves before the Lord, and he will lift you up (James 4:4-10).

God is longing to draw his people closer to him today, and to protect them from the onslaught of the enemy in a time when the forces of materialism and secularism are rampant in the world, and when the forces of darkness are gathering for the greatest ever conflict in the history of mankind. God cannot use his Church while there is so much worldliness and un-righteousness among its members, such a lack of trust and sheer blind unbelief. The word of the Lord to the Church today is the same as that with which Jesus began his ministry in Galilee, "Repent and believe, for the Kingdom of God is near."

13.

A Listening People

One of the greatest needs today is for the Church to be a listening people, responsive to God. The dangers confronting us in the world make it essential that the nations should be receiving the word of God for our times. They can only do this through the Church, whose task it is, as the body of Christ, to carry out the work of Christ in the world and to proclaim faithfully the word of our God in the hearing of the nations.

The Church is to be the watchman to the nations. This is the prophetic task. It must be the prophet to the world. That is the New Testament concept of the Church. It is for this reason that God is calling upon his Church, the believers in the Lord Jesus, to be a prophetic people. We need to study carefully both contemporary events and also the word of the Lord. But above all we need to be a listening people, that we may respond rightly to our God in these critical days. God will undoubtedly hold us responsible for coming events if disaster strikes our world and we have not faithfully witnessed to the word of God among the nations.

Every believer has a part – a vital part – to play in this prophetic task. It is not sufficient to leave it to those who hold official leadership positions within the churches today. God is calling the whole believing body of Christ to be a prophetic people, so that there may be a build-up in the faith of the Church, in her expectancy, and in the power of her witness to the world. God wants all his people to be a listening people, able to receive and to transmit his word.

He nevertheless gives the special task of hearing from him to those whom he has anointed with the ministry gift of the prophet. They have a special responsibility to be alert to what God is saying, so that they may draw the attention of the whole body of Christ to the word of God for our times, in order that the whole body may embrace the contemporary word of the Lord. It is, of course, absolutely essential that the leaders, to whom God has given the special responsibility of the prophetic task, should be especially sensitive to him in these critical days. If they neglect to stand in the counsel of the Lord or fail to hear him correctly and discern his word, disaster strikes.

Disaster struck Israel in the time of Joshua for this very same reason. Joshua and all the people of Israel were rejoicing greatly over the tremendous victory at Jericho. They were flushed with success. After forty years of wandering in the wilderness they had at last crossed Jordan and entered the Promised Land. The first city they had struck was Jericho. From the spiritual standpoint this city was the first-fruit of the land which was to be given to the Lord. It was for this reason that they were forbidden to take any of the plunder for themselves, as was usual with a conquering army when it overcame a city. One man disobeyed God in this respect and gave way to his own selfish avarice, taking and hiding some of the plunder in his tent.

It was not, however, just the sin of Achan that brought disaster upon Israel when they moved against the second city in Canaan at Ai. Joshua himself bore a large measure of the responsibility for the routing of his soldiers by the men of Ai. He listened to some of his own soldiers and did not listen to the Lord.

Joshua sent an advance party ahead of him to spy out the land and to report on the defences and strength of the city of Ai before moving against it. The reconnaissance party came back with a report that the defences were weak and that the army of the king of Ai was quite small and could easily be overcome. They gave this advice to Joshua: "Not all the people will have to go up against Ai. Send two or three thousand men to take it and do not weary all the people, for only a few men are there" (Joshua 7:3).

Joshua listened to this advice, and he allowed the reconnaissance party to dictate the strategy for the battle against Ai. He did not go before the Lord and stand in his counsel, seeking his word to set the strategy for this fresh campaign. He had not learned that God does not repeat himself, but has a fresh strategy for each fresh phase of the campaign. God had set the strategy for taking Jericho, which must have seemed utterly ridiculous and irrational to the leaders of Israel; but they knew Joshua was a man who was hearing from God, therefore they trusted the word he received. They were obedient to the strategy set by the Lord, and they therefore witnessed the miracle of the taking of Jericho, whose walls simply fell down before them.

Joshua was careless over Ai, evidently thinking that, according to his advance patrol, it would be easy. He sent three thousand men to take Ai and they were routed: a number of them were killed and the whole company were chased down the valley all the way back to their base camp near Jericho.

Joshua was distraught because he realized that word of this defeat would spread like wildfire throughout the countryside, and all the local tribes would come against Israel to annihilate them. Joshua even bemoaned the fact that they had crossed the Jordan into Canaan; he wished they had been content to stay on the east bank and not come in to possess the land. All day long he lay face downwards on the floor in front of the Ark of the Covenant, weeping and wailing and wallowing in self-misery. When at last God did speak to him it was a stern command to get up: "Stand up! What are you doing down on your face? Israel has sinned " (Joshua 7:10).

Joshua had to face up to the fact that he and all Israel had sinned before the Lord. When he resumed the campaign against Ai he did so having humbled himself before God, having listened to the Lord and having received from him a fresh strategy for the taking of this city. It was then that victory followed.

God is speaking to his people today and reminding us of the necessity for hearing from him. God does speak today as he did in ancient times, for the nature of God is unchanging. "Surely the sovereign Lord does nothing without revealing his plan to his servants the prophets" (Amos 3:7). There are many servants of the Lord among the nations today who are hearing from God, but whose voices are not being heard and heeded by the whole Church. Just as the prophets in ancient Israel were not to be found among the priests and rulers of the nation, so today we do not usually find those with a prophetic anointing among the acknowledged leadership in the Church. The two offices do not easily go together!

The prophet's message is rarely a popular one; it is often directed against the lack of faith and absolute trust in the Lord, the lack of obedience to his word that is all too often found among leaders as well as among the people. The prophets of ancient Israel were rarely applauded for their task. Hosea had a stern message to bring to both leaders and people of Israel:

Do not rejoice, O Israel; do not be jubilant like the other nations. For you have been unfaithful to your God; you love the wages of a prostitute at every threshing-floor.

Threshing-floors and winepresses will not feed the people; the new wine will fail them (Hosea 9:1 and 2).

Hosea then went on to prophesy disaster upon the nation of Israel and exile for her people:

> The days of punishment are coming. The days of reckoning are at hand. Let Israel know this.

The message was so unpopular that it aroused great hostility and suffering for the prophet. The measure of this can be seen from the comment with which Hosea followed the prophecy:

> Because your sins are so many and your hostility so great, the prophet is considered a fool, the inspired man a maniac.
>
> The prophet, along with my God, is the watchman over Ephraim, yet snares await him on all his paths, and hostility in the house of his God (Hosea 9:7 and 8).

God is speaking to men and women with prophetic insight in all the nations, and revealing to them the significance of the days in which we live and the urgent need for the contemporary world to hear the contemporary word of our God.

In July 1983 God spoke to me, saying that the time had come for those with prophetic insight from among the nations of the world to meet with one another to share what they had been hearing from him. From such a gathering would emerge a clear picture of the worldwide significance of contemporary events that would give renewed vision to the people of God and strength for the proclamation of his word to the nations.

*

I wrote down the actual words that I heard from the Lord:

> **"When you see this your heart will rejoice and you will flourish like grass; the hand of the Lord will be made known to his servants, but his fury will be shown to his foes "** *(Isaiah 66:14).*
>
> **This day I am fulfilling my word. Today I am calling forth my servants the prophets from every land to come together and seek my face that they may proclaim my word to the nations. I have not left myself without a witness in this generation. I have spoken to my servants and they shall speak my words to the people.**
>
> **Today you are to call them to come out from among the people and the nations and seek me together, that my word may be known among them and heard among the nations.**
>
> **Be strong and of good courage and you will see the unfolding of my will and you will go out with joy and will sing of the faithfulness of your God.**
>
> **You must find my prophets in every land and bring them together. I will show you the next step when they come together. I myself will be with you in this task.**

This was followed by other words of a personal nature that gave direction and encouragement to me. The task seemed both crazy and impossible, but the experience was so strong that I never doubted that God had spoken to me.

This word was subsequently shared, tested and confirmed with a number of those with prophetic ministries. The Lord later revealed that this gathering was to take place on Mount Carmel in Israel. We were led to a centre in an isolated location in a national park on the summit of Mount Carmel. We were given the timing for this event as the week prior to

Easter 1986, and that it should be followed by a pro-clamation of the word of God in Jerusalem during the Easter period, and in particular on the day when Christians celebrate the resurrection of the Lord Jesus. We were also shown that Christians from many nations would be in Jerusalem at that time, and would carry the word of God back to the leaders and people in their own lands.

Additionally we were shown that Maundy Thursday was of great significance in the gathering of believers in Jerusalem, for it was on that day that Jesus wept over the city of Jerusalem. As he came over the brow of the hill from Bethany and looked over the whole city laid out before him across the valley, he saw with prophetic insight what was going to happen to the city and its people. Not one stone would be left upon another. Even the Temple would be destroyed. The great walls of Jerusalem would be broken down and there would be a great slaughter of the people, and the remnant would be scattered across the nations of the world. This would begin centuries of suffering for the people of Israel, who would not be re-gathered to their land nor have the city of Jerusalem restored to their hands until the end of the age drew near.

As Jesus contemplated the city that he loved, on the day before his own crucifixion and rejection by the leaders of his people, he wept. He wept not for his own pain and suffering that was about to begin, but for the suffering of the people he loved and who had been called by God to be "a light unto the Gentiles". He wept because he saw the terrible times that were coming upon the city, and the brokenness of the people as the city was raped and pillaged by her enemies.

Jesus knew that the seal would be set upon those times on that very day when he would be arrested in the Garden of Gethsemane, and the people would reject God's own Messiah. Jesus' eyes filled with tears as he gazed upon the city from across the valley, looking at the beautiful Temple and the Golden Gate that he would never see again in his earthly ministry.

O Jerusalem, Jerusalem, you who killed the prophets and stoned those sent to you, how often I have longed to gather your children together as a hen gathers her chicks under her wings, but you were not willing. Look, your house is left to you desolate.

If you, even you, had only known on this day what would bring you peace – but it is hidden from your eyes. The days will come upon you when your enemies will build an embankment against you and encircle you and hem you in on every side. They will dash you to the ground, you and the children within your walls. They will not leave one stone on another, because you did not recognize the time of God's coming to you (Matthew 23:37 and 38, and Luke 19:41-44).

All this happened in the year AD 70, when the Romans took savage revenge upon the nation of Israel, after a fruitless rebellion by a people who were not hearing from their Lord, who had rebelled against God, who had rejected his Messiah and who in the words of Jesus "*did not recognize the time of God's coming* to them*". The city was destroyed. Half a million people in Judea were murdered. The nation was driven from the land, dispossessed from the inheritance of their fathers, and groups of survivors found refuge in many lands, being left to wander as refugees among the nations for nearly two thousand years.

The consequences of missing the timing of God are terrible. God expects his people to be able to discern the signs of the times. He sends many warning signs. He speaks to his prophets. He reveals to them what will happen if his warnings go unheeded and his word ignored.

God even pleads with his people to turn to him, to trust him and obey him. Finally, he withdraws his covering of protection and his people are left exposed to the enemy.

That was what happened to Jerusalem soon after the rejection and crucifixion of the Messiah.

14.

In Simple Trust

We are the most privileged generation for two thousand years! We live in the days of which Jesus and the prophets spoke. The signs of the times are clear for those who have eyes to see and who have some knowledge of the word of God.

God is fulfilling his promises. He is at the same time calling for fresh obedience and love and trust from his people. He is urging us to open our eyes, to understand what is taking place in the world today, and to perceive the significance of what he is doing, as well as to be alert to the growing menace of the enemy and the great dangers confronting us.

In our own generation the people of Israel, survivors from among the nations, have been re-gathered to the land, and the ancient city of Jerusalem has been restored to their hands according to the words of Jesus. "They will fall by the sword and will be taken as prisoners to all the nations. Jerusalem will be trampled on by the Gentiles until the times of the Gentiles are fulfilled" (Luke 21:24).

Jesus speaks of the return of the Jewish people to Jerusalem in the context of his discourse on the events surrounding the last days of this present age. It should be emphasized that the "end of the age" does not signify the end of the world. "An age" in biblical terms is simply a period of time denoting God's dealings with his people, and may be any number of years. Jesus was referring to the end of the age that was about to be established with the coming of the Holy Spirit at Pentecost. The end of an age is always a cataclysmic period, as was the end of the age for the northern kingdom of Israel in the year 722 BC, when Samaria fell to the Assyrians. There was a time of terrible suffering at the end of the following age in the year 587 BC, when Jerusalem fell to Nebuchadnezzar and the seventy years' exile in Babylon began. In the same way, the end of the age for the Jewish nation in AD 70 was, as Jesus predicted, another time of dreadful suffering, when the cruelty and atrocities committed by the Roman soldiers defy description.

It was for this reason that Jesus wept over Jerusalem. He foresaw the fearful consequences of their failure to understand the signs of the times and to be alert to what God was saying to them and doing in their generation.

Jeremiah had similarly wept tears over Jerusalem six hundred years earlier; he had foreseen its destruction by the Babylonians and had pleaded with the leaders, crying out among the people and calling them to repent, to turn away from their wicked ways and to put their trust in the Lord their God.

Long before the city was destroyed and the people slaughtered, the scenes of destruction were revealed vividly to the prophet – so vividly that he saw it as though it had already happened and he wept:

Since my people are crushed, I am crushed; I mourn, and horror grips me.

Oh, that my head were a spring of water and my eyes a fountain of tears! I would weep day and night for the slain of my people.

Let my eyes overflow with tears night and day without ceasing; for my virgin daughter – my people – has suffered a grievous wound, a crushing blow.

If I go into the country, I see those slain by the sword; if I go into the city, I see the ravages of famine. Both prophet and priest have gone to a land they know not (Jeremiah 8:21; 9:1; 14:17 and 18).

Jeremiah loved his people and he loved the ancient city of Jerusalem. It broke his heart to see the rebellion of the people, their hardness of heart and their refusal to hear and to heed the word of the Lord. He knew the end result of their spiritual blindness and deafness, and of the moral, social and political corruption that was gripping the nation. He knew that the word he brought from God would be unpopular. Inevitably it brought him great suffering. He was put in the stocks in the city streets and pelted by the populace. He was imprisoned. He was accused of being a traitor. He was even dropped down a filthy, muddy well and left to die, but was saved by some of his friends.

Despite all his suffering and the hatred that was generated by his preaching the word of the Lord in Jerusalem, Jeremiah could not keep quiet, for the word of the Lord burned within him. His own testimony is:

> I am ridiculed all day long; everyone mocks me. Whenever I speak, I cry out proclaiming violence and destruction. So the word of the Lord has brought me insult and reproach all day long.
>
> But if I say, "I will not mention him or speak any more in his name", his word is in my heart like a burning fire, shut up in my bones. I am weary of holding it in; indeed, I cannot (Jeremiah 20:7-9).

The most painful experience for Jeremiah must have been as the enemy armies drew near to lay siege to the doomed city, and still there was the same stubborn refusal to hear the word of the Lord and to repent. Jeremiah was told to stop praying for the deliverance of Jerusalem. Three times he was told not to pray for the people:

> So *do not pray for this people* nor offer any plea or petition for them; do not plead with me, for I will not listen to you (Jeremiah 7:16).

149

Do not pray for this people nor offer any plea or petition for them because I will not listen when they call to me in the time of their distress (Jeremiah 11:14).

Then the Lord said to me, "*Do not pray for the well-being of this people.* Although they fast, I will not listen to their cry; though they offer burnt offerings and grain offerings, I will not accept them. Instead, I will destroy them with the sword, famine and plague" (Jeremiah 14:11 and 12).

The "prophetic silence" is the most devastating announcement of judgement ever recorded. The silence of the prophet of God is deafening. It can be heard reverberating through the pages of the history of Israel more than two thousand five hundred years later. Through the silence the finger of God was writing "Ichabod" (glory departed) over a rebellious generation of his people. Through the silence, as the prophet's prayers ceased to go up from the streets of Jerusalem, there could be heard the tears of the Lord as he wept for his people. The Lord God, slow to anger and abounding in mercy, held out the covering of his loving protection to the people of Jerusalem almost to the end. His promise was sure:

If at any time I announce that a nation or kingdom is to be uprooted, torn down and destroyed, and if that nation I warned repents of its evil, then I will relent and not inflict on it the disaster I had planned (Jeremiah 18:7 and 8).

But the promises and the pleading of God fell upon deaf ears. Ezekiel, who prophesied in the same period, describes vividly how he saw God withdraw his presence from the city of Jerusalem shortly before Nebuchadnezzar's blood-thirsty hordes smashed through the city walls to rape, pillage and plunder. In a vision, Ezekiel saw how "the glory of the God of Israel went up from above the cherubim, where it had been, and moved to the threshold of the Temple" (Ezekiel 9:3). God's final act was to withdraw the covering of his own protection from over the city and leave it desolate to the ravages of the enemy.

Jesus also saw the glory of the presence of God and his covering of protection being removed from the city of Jerusalem in his own day, just as Ezekiel had in his day nearly six hundred years earlier. That is why Jesus wept over the city the day before his rejection by the whole house of Israel and his crucifixion, and that is the meaning of his words, "Look, your house is left to you desolate (Mattew 23:38)."

When the loving presence and covering protection of the Lord is withdrawn from a people they are left desolate. They are helpless before their enemies. The seeing of such a sight is the most fearful experience that any servant of the Lord may have.

Like Jeremiah, I have stood in the counsel of the Lord, and I have seen and bear testimony to the devastation that is coming upon the nations of the world unless there is repentance in this generation. The Lord is warning the nations of the inevitable end of the path upon which they are now treading. It leads to destruction – utter destruction!

I have seen, as vividly as though it has already taken place, the scenes of destruction that will fall upon the nations unless they heed the word of God for our times. But it is not God's will that this should happen. God loves the nations. The people are the creation of his own hand and he longs to save them. "For God so loved the world that he gave his one and only Son, that whoever believes in him shall not perish but have eternal life. For God did not send his Son into the world to condemn the world but to save the world through him" (John 3:16 and 17).

Never was there greater urgency that the nations should hear the words of the Lord Jesus, "Repent and believe, for the kingdom of God is at hand."

Never was there greater urgency that the word of salvation through Christ Jesus should be received by the nations. For this purpose God has been planting his Church in every nation and throughout every region and continent of the world. It is for this purpose today, in these days of mounting world crisis as the nations are being precipitated towards the inevitable destruction that will come upon them, that God is pouring out his Spirit afresh upon the nations and calling men to repentance. He is giving a fresh touch of his Holy Spirit to believers in the Lord Jesus in every land. He is raising a people of power, and calling them to a greater boldness and to fresh love and trust in his word.

God is pleading with the nations through his people:

> Turn to me and be saved, all you ends of the earth for I am God, and there is no other. By myself I have sworn, my mouth has uttered in all integrity a word that will not be revoked: before me every knee will bow; by me every tongue shall swear (Isaiah 45:22 and 23).

God *will* establish his Kingdom upon earth. His purposes are sure. His intention is that either the nations will be broken and subdued through judgement or they will come to him through willing repentance and be received in his love and mercy. But his word has been spoken and his ultimate purposes *will* be carried out. "All who have raged against him will come to him and be put to shame" (Isaiah 45:24).

God is raising his Church today as a prophetic people to proclaim his word with power and conviction to the nations. But he does not see the obedience and love and trust among his own people that is essential to meet the challenge of these times. So God is pleading with his Church, his own people, the body of Christ.

"When will you listen?", says the Lord to the Church. "I have sent you the prophets. I have sent you my word. I have given you my own beloved Son, but you do not listen to him or heed my word. You are a stiff-necked people, preoccupied with your own affairs and caught up in your own desires. You are a hindrance to my work in the world. My purpose is to save mankind, not to destroy; to save the nations, not to annihilate. But you do not understand my purposes or heed my warnings, therefore you will go into the pit with the nations unless you repent and turn to me."

The Lord is weeping over his Church today as Jesus wept over Jerusalem.

"Turn to me, O my people. See the tears in my eyes for you. Hear the love in my voice for you. I do not desire that judgement should come upon you. I long to embrace you in my arms and for you to experience the loving security of my embrace. Underneath are the everlasting arms of my love. But you must receive them. You must reach out to me as I am reaching out to you. Receive my love. Receive my Spirit as I breathe on you afresh today. I have given you the power of my Spirit. Repent and believe. Turn away from your faithless ways and put your trust in me. In me there is life and joy in abundance. Outside me there is only death and destruction."

God is calling upon his people to turn to him in childlike trust and simple belief. When he wanted to teach this lesson to his own disciples Jesus took a little child and set him in the midst of them, and said they must become like little children with eyes wide open in love and trust.

It is perhaps for this reason that God is showing special favour to the peoples of the newer nations today. It is there that the Spirit of God is moving mightily. It is there that the signs and wonders and miraculous happenings are everyday events. Miracles are part of the ordinary normal experience of the Church, not the abnormal.

I was speaking the other day about this with Bishop Ban It Chiu of Singapore. We were talking about the Holy Spirit revival that is sweeping South East Asia, including China. I said to him, "Do you often see signs and wonders?" He looked at me in amazement and said, "It would be a wonder if there were no signs!" He told me of a pastor working in mainland China who had kept his faith and remained close to the Lord Jesus, even through the violence of the cultural revolution. He had, of course, never been to Bible college or had any formal education, for even ordinary secular education was abolished during the cultural revolution. Teachers were violently abused, degraded and even murdered when the schools were closed and the students elevated above their teachers. This man had maintained his faith through the days of upheaval and today, when the climate of religious tolerance has made life easier for him, he is able freely to witness and to move from village to village and town to town, preaching the Gospel of the Lord Jesus.

Recently the pastor was called to a family in a village some distance away where a woman was dying. By the time he reached her she was already dead and had been laid out on a bier in front of the house, according to the Chinese custom in those parts. There were four Communist officials present who were taking details of the woman's death. When they learned that she was a Christian they began abusing members of the family, and they turned upon the pastor and railed upon him, taunting him that if he was supposed to worship a God who was raised from the dead he should do the same for this woman; he should pray for her and raise her from the dead.

The pastor, being a man of simple faith, laid his hands on the dead woman and prayed for her. Immediately she sat up and clapped her hands. The four Communist officials were petrified. They ran terrified up the street. The woman said she had just been to Heaven and she had got something very wonderful to tell them, but first of all she insisted on cooking a meal for them and gathering the whole family before her.

By this time news of the event had spread right through the village and four hundred people gathered around the house to hear the woman's testimony. When they heard her words and the challenge of the Gospel from her pastor, all of them committed their lives to the Lord Jesus, including three of the Communist officials.

In simple trust. This is the way the Lord expects his people to come to him today. "Do not fear the enemy", he is saying to us, as he said to those who came to him in simple trust in the time of King Jehoshaphat in Jerusalem. They gathered there in a time of international crisis, when a combined army from a number of nations around Israel was threatening to invade and overwhelm them. Humanly speaking the situation was desperate, as the tiny army of Israel was no match for the combined forces of the enemy. But Jehoshaphat remembered a promise that God had given to his ancestor Solomon, "If my people who are called by my name will humble themselves and pray and seek my face and turn from their wicked ways, then I will hear from heaven and will forgive their sin and will heal their land" (2 Chronicles 7:14).

Jehoshaphat called the people to Jerusalem, to come in penitence before the Lord their God, and to cry out to him for the nation. They came, in simple trust, men, women and children. The king summed up their feelings in a beautiful prayer: "For we have no power to face this vast army that is attacking us. We do not know what to do, but our eyes are upon you." The answer came immediately when the Spirit of the Lord came upon Jehaziel the prophet: "Do not be afraid or discouraged because of this vast army. For the battle is not yours, but God's" (2 Chronicles 20:12 and 15).

The Lord is saying these same words to his people today.

"The battle is not yours but mine", says the Lord. Turn to me and be saved. Put your trust in me, for I alone am able to overcome the forces of destruction that are moving across the face of the earth. O my people, my people, put your trust in me and abide in me. You are my prophetic people and I long to work through you mightily, for I love you.

Fount Paperbacks

Fount is one of the leading paperback publishers of religious books and below are some of its recent titles.

- [ ] THE WAY OF ST FRANCIS Murray Bodo £2.50
- [ ] GATEWAY TO HOPE Maria Boulding £1.95
- [ ] LET PEACE DISTURB YOU Michael Buckley £1.95
- [ ] DEAR GOD, MOST OF THE TIME YOU'RE QUITE NICE Maggie Durran £1.95
- [ ] CHRISTIAN ENGLAND VOL 3 David L Edwards £4.95
- [ ] A DAZZLING DARKNESS Patrick Grant £3.95
- [ ] PRAYER AND THE PURSUIT OF HAPPINESS Richard Harries £1.95
- [ ] THE WAY OF THE CROSS Richard Holloway £1.95
- [ ] THE WOUNDED STAG William Johnston £2.50
- [ ] YES, LORD I BELIEVE Edmund Jones £1.75
- [ ] THE WORDS OF MARTIN LUTHER KING Coretta Scott King (Ed) £1.75
- [ ] BOXEN C S Lewis £4.95
- [ ] THE CASE AGAINST GOD Gerald Priestland £2.75
- [ ] A MARTYR FOR THE TRUTH Grazyna Sikorska £1.95
- [ ] PRAYERS IN LARGE PRINT Rita Snowden £2.50
- [ ] AN IMPOSSIBLE GOD Frank Topping £1.95
- [ ] WATER INTO WINE Stephen Verney £2.50

All Fount paperbacks are available at your bookshop or newsagent, or they can be ordered by post from Fount Paperbacks, Cash Sales Department, G.P.O. Box 29, Douglas, Isle of Man, British Isles. Please send purchase price, plus 15p per book, maximum postage £3. Customers outside the U.K. send purchase price, plus 15p per book. Cheque, postal or money order. No currency.

NAME (Block letters) _____

ADDRESS _____

_____